Special Times

Honoring Our Jewish
and Christian Heritages
For Grades 1 and 2

Betty Jo Middleton

Patricia Hoertdoerfer, Developmental Editor

Unitarian Universalist Association

This program was designed and written in collaboration with the Heritages from Judaism and Christianity Curriculum Team: Elizabeth Anastos, Nannene Gowdy, Nina D. Grey, Robert L'H. Miller, Mary Ann Moore, Marjorie Skwire, and Stephen Washburn.

Copyright © 1994 by the Unitarian Universalist Association, 25 Beacon Street, Boston, MA 02108. All rights reserved. Printed in USA.

Permission is granted to photocopy resources for use within this program only.

ISBN 1-55896-281-6

04 03 02 01 / 9 8 7 6 5 4 3

Production Editor: Brenda Wong
Editorial Assistant: Debra Anderson
Text Designer: Suzanne Morgan
Cover Designer: Bruce Jones

Acknowledgments

Every effort has been made to trace the owner(s) of copyright material. We regret any omission and will, upon written notice, make the necessary correction(s) in subsequent printings.

Special thanks to:

Mary Ann Moore for "New Friends and Old," Session 1.

Mary Lib-Whitney for "A New Year," Session 3; "A Winter Day," Session 16; "A Hosanna Day," Session 20.

Kirsti Adkins for the "Advent List of Activities," Resource 15.

Barbara Marshman for "The Lord's Prayer," Resource 25.

Heather McDonald for "Thanksgiving" closing words in Session 10.

Larry Phillips who arranged and typeset the music in this program.

We gratefully acknowledge the use of the following material:

"Elizabeth Blackwell" from *People Like Us*, by Elizabeth Gillis. Copyright © 1989 by the Society of the First and Second Church, Boston, MA. Reprinted by permission.

"Whitney Young" from *A Stream of Living Souls*, by Denise Tracy. Copyright © 1987 by Delphi Resources, 421 S. Clinton Avenue, Oak Park, IL 60302. Reprinted by permission.

"Amos Peck Seaman" by Mary Hamilton in Session 7 and background information in Session 10 from *Exploring Our Roots*, by Margaret K. Gooding. Copyright © 1988. Reprinted by permission of the Canadian Unitarian Council, Toronto, Canada.

"The Story of the Birth of Jesus," by Aloyse Hume from *Winter Festivals and Celebrations*. Copyright © 1976. Reprinted by permission of the Church of the Larger Fellowship, Boston, MA.

"Rosh Ha-Shanah Eve," by Harry Philip, from *Poems for Jewish Holidays*, by Myra C. Livingston. Copyright © 1986 by Harry Philip. Reprinted by permission.

"The Story of Purim" in Session 17 and "Recipe for Matzoh" in Session 19 from *Jewish Holiday Fun*, by Judith Hoffman Corwin. Copyright © 1987 by Judith Hoffman Corwin. Reprinted by permission of Simon & Schuster, Inc.

"The Simple, Old Man: Aaron David Gordon," "The Mother of Israel: Henrietta Szold," and "The Hora Dance Steps" in Session 22 from *A Kid's Catalog of Israel*, by Chaya Burstein. Copyright © 1988 by the Jewish Publishing Society. Reprinted by permission.

"Recipe for Haroset" from *Festival of Freedom: The Story of Passover*, by Maida Silverman and Carolyn S. Ewing. Text copyright © 1988 by Maida Silverman. Illustrations copyright © 1988 by Carolyn S. Ewing. Reprinted by permission of Simon & Schuster, Inc.

"The Ten Commandments" in Resource 28 from *My Very Own Shavuot*, by Judyth Saypol and Madeline Wikler. Copyright © 1982 by Kar-Ben Copies, Inc., Rockville, MD. Reprinted by permission of Kar-Ben Copies, Inc.

"The Four Questions" in Resource 24 from *My Very Own Haggadah*, by Judith Saypol and Madeline Wikler. Copyright © 1974 by Kar-Ben Copies, Inc., Rockville, MD. Reprinted by permission of Kar-Ben Copies, Inc.

We gratefully acknowledge the use of the following songs:

Brotman-Marshfield for "Dayenu" (words) and Jan Evans-Tiller for "We've Got the Whole World in Our Hands" (words).

"Love Is a Circle," by Phyllis Unger Hiller from the album Ramo. Copyright © 1971 by Phyllis Unger Hiller. Used with permission of Oak Hill Music Publishing Co., Nashville, TN 37212.

"Standing Like a Tree," by Betsy Rose. Words and music copyright © 1988 by Paper Crane Music. Used by permission.

"Alleluia Sing!" by Shelley Jackson Denham. Words and music copyright © 1988 by Shelley Jackson Denham. Used by permission.

Contents

Introduction 1

Special Times Planning Calendar 7

Dates of Jewish and Christian Holy Days 10

1.   A Time to Say "Hello"—Ingathering 11
   First Sunday

2.   A Time for Worship—Shabbat and Sabbath 17
   Second Sunday/Anytime

3.   A Time for the Year to Begin Again—Rosh Hashanah 21
   September/October

4.   A Time for Forgiveness—Yom Kippur 26
   September/October, following Rosh Hashanah

5.   A Time for Harvest—Sukkot 30
   October, following Yom Kippur

6.   A Time for Learning—Simhat Torah 33
   October

7.   A Time for Heroes and Heroines—All Saints' Day 36
   October/November/Moveable

8.   A Time to Bless the Animals—St. Francis Day 42
   October/Anytime

9.   A Time to Remember Those Who Have Died—All Souls' Day 46
   November

10. A Time to Give Thanks—Thanksgiving Day 50
    October (Canada)/November (US)

11. A Time for Freedom of Worship—Hanukkah 56
    November/December

12. A Time for Getting Ready—Advent 60
    November/December

| 13 | A Time for Joy to be Born—Christmas Eve | 64 |

December

| 14 | A Time for Giving Gifts—Epiphany | 68 |

January

| 15 | A Time to Plant Trees—Tu Bishvat | 72 |

January/February

| 16 | A Time to Say "I Love You"—Valentine's Day | 76 |

February

| 17 | A Time to Celebrate Victory Over Discrimination—Purim | 81 |

February/March

| 18 | A Time to Help Others—Lent | 85 |

February/March

| 19 | A Time to Be Free from Slavery—Pesah | 89 |

March/April

| 20 | A Time for the Teachings of Jesus—Palm Sunday | 95 |

March/April

| 21 | A Time for Rebirth—Easter | 99 |

March/April

| 22 | A Time to Return Home—Yom ha-Atzmaut | 104 |

May/Moveable

| 23 | A Time to Do Right—Shavuot | 109 |

May/June

| 24 | A Time for Wondering About God—Always | 112 |

Anytime

| 25 | A Time When Each Person Is Special—Everybody's Birthday | 115 |

Anytime

| 26 | A Time to Say "Good-bye"—Closing Sunday | 118 |

Last Sunday

Bibliography 122

Index to Resources 125

Leader Evaluation Form 159

Introduction

Special Times is a year-long religious education program for children who are six and seven years old or in first and second grades. It acquaints children with the Jewish and Christian heritages out of which our Unitarian Universalist faith has grown, and engages them in celebrations of Jewish and Christian holidays and other "special times," such as the Shabbat/Sabbath, Thanksgiving, and everybody's birthday.

It consists of 26 sessions approximately 60 minutes long. Each session stands alone: arts and crafts projects, for example, do not continue from week to week. Continuity is provided by the theme, the ritual of the format, the leadership team, and an environment that provides ongoing learning centers.

Goals

Special Times will help children appreciate our Jewish and Christian heritages and recognize the special quality of time set apart for worship and celebration. Children will also better understand how important ritual, celebration, tradition, and wonder are to all peoples.

As children participate in *Special Times*, they will begin to see and honor the diversity and particularity as well as the unity and universality of our Jewish and Christian heritages. Children's religious education and faith development are enhanced as they become aware of the connections between Unitarian Universalism and the Jewish and Christian traditions. Throughout the sessions of *Special Times,* stories give children opportunities to develop an understanding of the abiding religious themes.

The messages of *Special Times* are intended to enhance the Unitarian Universalist community and affirm young people in their religious meaning-making. Of course, this curriculum as any curriculum is a springboard, a starting place. Teachers are invited to adapt sessions using their own creative imaginations and the special talents of their congregation.

Relationship to Unitarian Universalist Principles

Special Times is based on the living tradition that draws from many sources, most specifically Jewish and Christian teachings, but also the "direct experience of that transcending mystery and wonder, . . . which moves us to . . . an openness to the forces that create and uphold life," and "words and deeds of prophetic women and men. . . . Wisdom from the world's religions. . . . Humanist teachings . . . "

All the principles of the Unitarian Universalist Association are addressed by this program, particularly:

- The inherent worth and dignity of every person
- Justice, equity, and compassion in human relations
- Acceptance of one another and encouragement to spiritual growth in our congregations
- The rights of conscience
- The goal of world community with peace, liberty, and justice for all.

Leaders will recognize Unitarian Universalist values in the activities and subject matter of the program, even when they are not explicitly stated.

Structure of the Sessions

Each session includes a title/theme, goals, a materials list, preparation guidelines, background information for leaders, and a session plan, which, in most sessions, includes the following:

Gathering: A time to welcome participants.

Focusing: A time to initiate the theme or focus of the session.

Conversation and Story: A time for interaction within the group as the participants explore through story what they know and think about the ideas presented.

Song: A time to sing in celebration of the event or holiday.

Activities: A time to help the children develop new or broader understandings of the theme by thinking, seeing, hearing, and doing.

Closing Circle: A time to bring the session to a close with a short ritual of candle or chalice lighting and a brief reflection on the theme of the session. If your group does not participate in a worship service before the session, you may want to have a short Opening Circle as well.

The session structure is based on an adaptation of the shared praxis model of teaching as explicated by religious educators Paulo Freire and Thomas Groome, and on educator John Dewey's view of education as "experience reflected upon." In each session the children are asked to contribute ideas related to their experiences of the religious themes of special times. Then new information is presented and explored which they can then integrate into their own thinking and doing.

Sequence of Sessions

The table of contents lists the appropriate time of year to hold each session. Only two of these are fixed—the Ingathering and the Closing sessions are intended for use only at those times. Some sessions will say "September/October" or "April/May." Others may say "Anytime" or "Moveable," or specify several appropriate times. For example, you may choose to use Session 25, the birthday session, at the beginning of the year to build community or at the end of the year to celebrate each person and your year together.

Careful planning before the program starts will facilitate your week-to-week scheduling in a number of ways: coordinating your sessions with the church calendar, ordering special materials, arranging for guests, finding books and supplies. As you begin your planning, create your own calendar using the blank *Special Times* Planning Calendar, which follows this introduction. Fill in the Sundays your religious education program will be in session, the dates of special events such as family services and celebrations, the actual date of each holiday, and the names of leaders and/or assistants for each session, and then hang it in your classroom.

Choices Time

Choices Time is built into almost every session to provide children with additional opportunities for exploring the themes of the program. Choices Time may also include a snack time in some sessions.

Special Corners, which are learning centers to be used during Choices Time, are easily created and help to provide continuity for the year's program. These corners may include the following:

Reading Corner: We have suggested a number of books pertinent to the overall theme and to specific sessions, but many others are available. Picture books with brief texts are good for this center, even though some of the children will read at a higher level.

Craft Center: Paper, envelopes, markers, crayons, glue, and other art materials on a cart or in an accessible cupboard may be used to make cards related to the session themes or for other purposes.

Gardening Window: A sunny window sill or a table near a window, flower pots or cans, a little potting soil, and some purchased seeds and/or seeds from foods we eat (avocado, for example) create a simple plant center that will keep the children in touch with the earth throughout the year. If your climate permits, you may wish to make this an outdoor option.

Moving About: The planned activities within each session offer opportunities for children to move about. Depending on the physical setting of your building, you may be able to take the children outdoors, either together or in small groups, for free play, coordinated games, or walks. If you have space indoors for active play, take advantage of it to allow restless bodies to work off some energy.

The Group

This program is intended primarily for first and second graders. It may be used, however, with other age groupings that best meet a congregation's needs—usually within the ages of six to eight years. Ten to twelve children with two leaders is ideal, but the program can be adapted for other size groups.

Parent Involvement

At this age, children learn values from their parents while beginning to be influenced more and more by teachers and friends. As a result, they feel most comfortable when parents and school or parents and church reinforce one another. Thus, parental involvement will contribute to the success of this program, and we have provided some suggestions for involving parents and other family members in the program.

Leaders

We strongly recommend two on-going leaders for this program, with perhaps a song leader, on-call assistants for more complicated projects and outdoor walks, and a regular substitute. Team leadership provides a richer experience for children and adults alike. Rotating leadership (when two or more leaders take turns but do not work together) is not recommended; such an arrangement makes it difficult for children to develop positive, trusting relationships with the leaders.

Working with other adults in a team helps to keep leaders from feeling isolated from the adult congregation. Planning together is especially important in this program, where the leaders are responsible for deciding when each session will be used, and fulfilling their responsibilities accordingly.

Intentional preparation and deliberate evaluation will enhance the flow of each session and your ease in leadership. Here are a few preparation tips:

1. Arrive 15-20 minutes before starting time to set up Reading Corner books, Craft Center supplies, and resources and materials for that particular session.

2. Greet the children individually as they arrive, give them symbol stickers appropriate for the session theme to decorate calendars and a UU poster, and then direct them to resources.

3. Remain 10-15 minutes after each session for the Evaluation and Planning time. Take time to evaluate your experience of that session with your co-leader and to plan the next session including each leader's responsibilities. Commitment to this activity will enhance your growth as an RE teacher and UU leader.

Characteristics of First and Second Graders

"Children are naturally curious about the really profound mysteries and deeply appreciative of universal and enduring values," writes Edith Hunter in *Conversations with Children*. This is perhaps especially true of six and seven year olds, who are deeply interested in birth, growing, death, and how things came to be.

Six and seven year olds are aware of their growing capabilities and autonomy. They have gained many skills in their brief lifespan and they want us to respect their experiences. Six and seven year olds enjoy physical activity, but they are now able to concentrate on a particular task for longer periods of time. They love ritual and order.

They like stories and want to know "if that really happened." Often adults can say only, "This is the story. . . . " Children like participating in stories and playing different characters and roles. They like to make things and to gather information. In addition to stories, children need arts and crafts, games, movement, and music to draw out their imagination. They want to know "Why?" about everything, and learning the origins of celebrations appeals to them.

Children at this age want to be "good" and to be told that they are doing well. They need opportunities to speak and be heard. They want and need opportunities to be responsible for themselves and to the group.

Environment

The meeting space should be large enough to accommodate the number of children in your group for the variety of activities in the program. You will need a regular gathering place for conversations and stories, preferably on a rug or in a circle of chairs. Table space for crafts is needed. Corners and niches in the room can hold the Special Corners, which will be needed at Choices Time. A window sill or a table near a sunny window is suggested for the Gardening Window. Perhaps a rolling cart, which can be brought into the room, can be the Craft Center or Reading Corner. Items made by the children will help to make the room a rich environment for learning.

Calendars

The four calendars—Jewish, Christian, Unitarian Universalist, and birthday—serve to integrate the relationships of the individual to his/her Unitarian Universalist faith and its Jewish and Christian heritages around the theme of special times. The four calendars are a visual focal point each Sunday as well as a starting point for discussion on the various themes of each session.

One activity to enhance these four relationships and stimulate religious learning is matching symbol stickers to holiday dates and special times. Children are invited each session to decorate the special time on the appropriate calendar with a variety of stickers. Symbol stickers also can be used to decorate the Unitarian Universalist poster highlighting the special time of the morning. The *"Special Times* celebrates _____ _____ today" sign on the Unitarian Universalist poster can be displayed on the classroom door each Sunday to communicate to parents, visitors, and the congregation the themes of the class throughout the year.

A wide range of inexpensive stickers is available commercially. Other stickers come in mailings from environmental, charitable, and commercial groups, and may be used with or without trimming away promotional wording. Jewish holiday stickers are available in several major chain card shops and at Jewish supply and bookstores. You may wish to purchase Paul E. Kennedy's *Fun With Jewish Stencils* (Toronto, Ontario, and Mineola, NY). The price is $1 in the United States.

Stories

Stories and the conversations and discussions that surround them are an integral part of each session. The stories chosen for this curriculum focus on the various themes identified in each session that honor our Jewish and Christian heritages or celebrate a special time common to all participants in the program. Children ages 6 and 7 love stories and become engaged in story ideas and characters that are relevant to their experiences and told or read in the appropriate age-level language. Please note that for Sessions 2, 9, 15, 24, and 25 you will need to obtain a copy of a children's book. Before these sessions, familiarize yourself with the story so you are able to read or tell it to the children with ease. After telling the story in each session, pause and invite children to tell you what they heard. Then engage them in discussing the specific questions included in the curriculum.

Six and seven year olds are capable of engaging in meaningful and productive discussions.

The length of their discussions will vary depending on the maturity of the participants and the effectiveness of the adult leadership. Some hints for leading discussions:

1. Keep the discussion moving. Raise a question or an idea and ask for responses. When one child has finished, move on to the next child.

2. Pay attention to the children's active participation and be ready to move on to the next topic or activity when they show signs of restlessness or lack of interest.

3. Be a model for good listening and speaking skills. Encourage the children to practice these skills daily.

Songs

Many songs are included in this program. Most of the songs are familiar and come from other religious education curricula, connecting the children to other experiences they have had in the church. We encourage you to engage the children in singing. If you do not have musical skills, recruit someone from your congregation to assist with teaching and leading songs with the children—a member of the choir, a folk singer, or one who can accompany the children with a guitar or autoharp. Several of the songs suggested are in two UUA publicatons, Signature Songbook 3 and *Bible Songs on Timeless Themes* (songbook and cassette tape). Others are in *Wee Sing-Around the Campfire*, an inexpensive songbook and cassette tape set, and *Songs for High Holidays* (Jewish), a cassette tape. All the cassette tapes are of children singing the songs, and are particularly good to use as sing-alongs. Use the cassette tapes for familiarizing the children with the songs and for singing along until they know them. Order in advance.

From the UUA Bookstore
Singing the Living Tradition. Boston, MA: UUA, 1993.
Signature Collection Songbook 3. Boston, MA: UUA, 1990.

Bible Songs on Timeless Themes, songbook and cassette tape, Eugene B. Navias, editor. Boston, MA: UUA, 1991.

From other publishers
Wee Sing-Around the Campfire, songbook and cassette tape, by Pamela Conn Beall and Susan Hagen Nipp. Los Angeles: Price/Sloan/Stern Publishers, Inc.
Songs for High Holidays, cassette tape, by Frances T. Goldman and Friends, Mason Stevens, Producer. Rockville, MD: Kar-Ben Copies, Inc.

Sample Planning Calendar

S E P T E M B E R	8 INGATHERING LUCY/JANET SAM, ASST.	15 ROSH HASHANAH LUCY/JANET	22 YOM KIPPUR LUCY/PARENT	29 SHABBAT/ SABBATH LUCY/PARENT JOHN, MUSIC
O C T O B E R	6 SIMHAT TORAH JANET/PARENT SAM, ASST.	13 THANKSGIVING LUCY/JANET	20 ST. FRANCIS LUCY/JANET	27 ALL SAINTS LUCY/PARENT

Session	Date	Theme	Leaders
1	Sept. 8	Ingathering	Lucy/Janet/Sam
2	Sept. 15	Rosh Hashanah	Lucy/Janet
3	Sept. 22	Yom Kippur	Lucy/Parent
4	Sept. 29	Shabbat/Sabbath	Lucy/Parent/John
5	Oct. 6	Simhat Torah	Janet/Parent/Sam
6	Oct. 13	Thanksgiving (Canda)	Janet/Lucy

Special Times Planning Calendar

SEPTEMBER				
OCTOBER				
NOVEMBER				
DECEMBER				

Special Times Planning Calendar

JANUARY				
FEBRUARY				
MARCH				
APRIL				

Special Times Planning Calendar

MAY				
JUNE				

Dates of Jewish and Christian Holy Days

Jewish Holy Days, 2000-2006

Holidays begin at sundown on the preceding day.

Rosh Hashanah
Tishri 1 and 2 (begins at sundown Elul 29)
September and October

2000: September 3
2001: September 18
2002: September 7
2003: September 27
2004: September 16
2005: October 4

Hanukkah
Kislev 25

2000: December 22
2001: December 10
2002: November 30
2003: December 20
2004: December 9
2005: December 26

Purim
2001: March 9
2002: February 26
2003: March 18
2004: March 7
2005: March 25
2006: March 14

Pesah
2001: April 8
2002: March 28
2003: April 17
2004: April 6
2005: April 24
2006: April 13

Shavuot
2001: May 28
2002: May 17
2003: June 6
2004: May 26
2005: June 13
2006: June 2

Christian Holy Days, 2001-2005
Easter
2001: April 15
2002: March 31
2003: April 20
2004: April 11
2005: March 27

1. A Time to Say "Hello"— Ingathering

Goals for Participants

- To become acquainted or re-acquainted with each other and their leaders.
- To feel welcomed, valued, and a sense of belonging to this group in this Unitarian Universalist congregation.
- To begin discovering what they will learn and celebrate in this year of *Special Times* together.

Materials

- Thick and fine markers and crayons in a variety of colors
- Pens and pencils
- Scissors, glue, and masking tape
- 9 x 12" and 12 x 18" construction paper in a variety of colors
- Stickers of the flaming chalice
- Special Corners materials of your choice
- Chalice, candle, and matches

Preparation

- Read the Introduction to the program and as many of the sessions as possible to familiarize yourself with the content and format of the sessions as well as the materials you will need to obtain in advance.

- Gather a selection of books from the Bibliography that are appropriate reading for the children, and have them available on a library table in the Reading Corner. Include your favorite books on any of the themes as well as the following books:
  Will I Have a Friend?, by Miriam Cohen
  Frog and Toad Are Friends, by Arnold Lobel
  A Picture Book of Jewish Holidays, by David Adler
  Book of Bible Stories, by Tomie de Paola
  Ring of Earth: A Child's Book of Seasons, by Jane Yolen
  I'm in Charge of Celebrations, by Byrd Baylor

- Recruit a photographer with an instant camera to take pictures of each child, or ask one of the leaders or assistants to do this.

- Gather all necessary supplies and resources for activities and Special Corners.

- Purchase stickers appropriate to the themes of the next several weeks.

- Photocopy and enlarge the circle calendars in Resources 1, 2, 3, and 4. Cut out each drawing and glue it on cardboard.

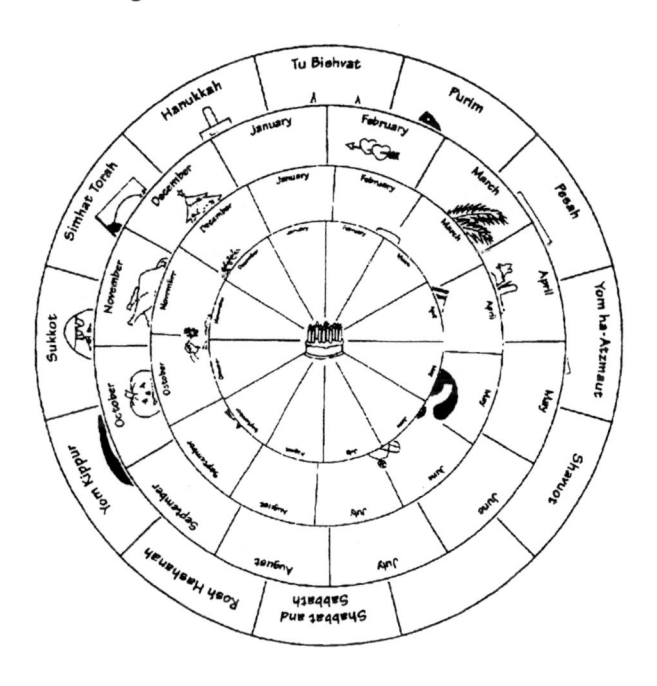

Session 1: A Time to Say "Hello"

Make a small hole in the center of each calendar. Insert a brass fastener through the holes, attaching the Birthday Calendar on top of the UU Calendar on top of the Christian Calendar on top of the Jewish Calendar. Keep the fasteners loose enough for the calendar wheels to rotate.

After you have prepared the calendar wheel, take the wheel apart and display the four calendars on the bulletin board or wall.

- Make a large colorful poster that includes the words "Unitarian Universalist" and the name of your congregation at the top. Make a sign, "*Special Times* celebrates today *Ingathering*," to fit on the poster. Hang the poster on the wall or bulletin board before the children arrive. This poster can be used later as a door sign to let parents know the theme of the week.

> **Unitarian Universalist First Parish**
>
> *Special Times* celebrates today *Ingathering*

- Make name tags for each child and leader.

- Learn the songs, "There is No One in the World Like Me" and "Make New Friends," in this session and be prepared to teach them to the children. Write the lyrics on newsprint or the chalkboard to help the children learn the words.

- Arrange your meeting room before Sunday morning if possible. Plan seating in a circle of chairs or pillows on the floor. Designate wall space or a bulletin board for the large calendars and the "About Me" posters that the children will create. Arrange tables for projects and Special Corners for Choices Time.

Background

This session engages the children in stories, songs, and expressive activities for recognizing their own specialness and experiencing a sense of belonging to a religious community that celebrates with many special times. This session concludes with a chalice-lighting ritual in a Closing Circle (as all sessions of this curriculum do). The chalice lighting symbolism reinforces the children's understanding of something special inside each person—something worth celebrating—here in our classroom and in our Unitarian Universalist congregation.

Session Plan

Gathering   Varies

As the children gather, help them feel welcomed and comfortable in their new surroundings on this first Sunday. If possible, greet each child by name. Direct them to the name tag materials and offer help where needed in finding and decorating their nametags. Invite them to browse among the Special Corners in the room—books, games, puzzles, and so forth. Ask your photographer to begin taking pictures of each child during this time.

Focusing   15 minutes

When all the children have arrived, invite them to join you in a circle on the rug or on chairs. Begin by introducing yourself again, then go around the circle, asking each child to tell her or his name and what their favorite special time is. Most will probably say their birthday. Let them talk about their own special times before leading them into religious celebrations. Repeat each person's name several times during this process to help both leaders and children remember one another's names.

Say something like, "This is a special place—this is our UU circle. What do the two U's stand for?" Invite responses from the children. Help them to learn that the two U's stand for "Unitarian Universalist," the name of their own congregation. Draw attention to the poster on the wall or bulletin board, saying something like, "Do you know why this is a very special circle? And do you know there is no other circle exactly like it in the whole wide world?"

Invite responses from the children. Then say, "It's because there are no other children in the world exactly like you. *You are special!* No other single child is exactly like _____ and _____ (say each child's name aloud). Let's sing a song about that; it's called 'There is No One in the World Like Me.'"

Teach them the song. Ask them to stand up and sing the song pointing to themselves every time they sing the word "me." After you have sung the song twice, ask the children to change the last word to "you" and point to a person next to them as they sing the word "you." Sing the song two more times.

When you have completed the song, ask the children to sit down again in the circle.

Conversation and Story   20 minutes

Ask the children to look at the four circle calendars on the wall, drawing their attention to the specially marked dates. Ask if they can find the calendar for birthdays and follow with the question, "*Are* birthdays special? Why?"

After listening to their responses, continue, "On one Sunday we will celebrate everybody's birthday! Let's find out when your birthdays are, and mark them on our Birthday Calendar." Write each child's name and birthdate on the Birthday Calendar.

Continue by saying something like, "We have also marked the times of the year when the seasons change—from summer to fall, fall to winter, winter to spring, and spring to summer. Many of our holidays are connected with the changes of the seasons.

"Now, let's look at our Unitarian Universalist calendar. We have marked special Sundays that we celebrate in our religious education program and in our Unitarian Universalist congregation." Invite the children to name and talk about these special times during the Unitarian Universalist year. Invite a child to place a flaming chalice sticker on the UU Calendar where it says "Ingathering Sunday."

Then draw the children's attention to the two larger calendars: the Jewish Calendar and the Christian Calendar. Ask the children if they recognize any of the symbols on either calendar. Invite them to name the special days—special times—represented by the symbols that they know.

Leaders then name some of the other symbols and special times which the children may not be familiar with. Then put the Christian Calendar inside the Jewish Calendar. Pause and encourage any connection and/or comments on the special times on these two calendars.

Then place the Unitarian Universalist Calendar inside the Christian Calendar. Again, pause and encourage the children to compare the special times on all three calendars. Then place the Birthday Calendar inside the UU Calendar and pause for comments.

Then say something like, "There are many special times in our year which are not here. We'll find out something about all of these and many more, and we will celebrate them, too, throughout our year together.

"We will also learn about the special time that comes each week—Sunday—when we come here to worship and learn as Unitarian Universalists. The Christians worship on Sunday or the Sabbath. The Jews worship on Saturday or the Shabbat. Other times are special, too. For instance, today is a special time. What do you think is special about today?"

Allow time for responses, like "It is the first time we have been here since before vacation," or "It is the first time we have been in this room." You might say, "It's good to be with our old friends again, isn't it? And to make new friends, too! Here is a story about new friends and old."

Read the story, "New Friends and Old."

After the story, ask:
- Have any of you felt like Jason? Tell us about it.

- What happened when you were playing with a friend like Alexandra and Emily and someone asked to join you?
- Is it sometimes hard to let someone new in? Why?

Song   5-10 minutes

Say something like, "Let's sing a song about making new friends and keeping old friends. Maybe you already know it."

Sing the song through once, then invite the children to join in. After singing it a few times, try singing it as a round.

Activities   10 minutes

Give each child a 12 x 18" sheet of construction paper and markers or crayons. Have glue and scissors available. Invite the children to make an "About Me" poster.

Say, "Make a poster which tells us something about you—your picture, your name, how old you are, your favorite foods, your favorite holiday, what you most like to do. You might want to glue the photo taken earlier by the photographer onto your poster. Do you have a pet? You could draw a picture of your pet, or print its name. You can put your family on your poster, your friends, schools, anyone or anything you like. You may want to show all this with pictures, or you may want to use words. Or both pictures and words. If you need help, ask me or one of the other leaders to help you. When your posters are finished, we will hang them up on the wall." Indicate the wall space or bulletin board where you will hang them. Leaders should also make an "About Me" poster.

Celebrate each poster as you hang it on the wall or bulletin board. Leave them up in your room for a couple of months as an additional aid to leaders and children in getting to know one another.

Choices Time   Varies

Tell the children that each week there will be a time when they may choose their own activities from one of the Special Corners you have created—the Reading Corner, Game Table, Gardening Window, and any special choices of the day. This may also be a good time to serve snacks if that is a custom in your church school.

Allow about 5 minutes before the Closing Circle for everyone to help clean up and put everything back in order.

Closing Circle   5 minutes

Gather the children in the circle, light the candle or chalice, and invite everyone to sit quietly for a moment and look at the flame. Then say something like, "Our special time together this morning is coming to an end. We light our chalice for the special times we have had today and for the new friends we have made. When we come back next week, we'll celebrate (name next week's special time)."

Close by singing the song "Make New Friends" once more. Ask a child to blow out the candle, saying, "We'll take turns lighting and blowing out the candle. Good-bye, until our special time together next week!"

If you want the children to use their name tags at the next session, ask them to take them off and put them in a designated place.

Evaluation and Planning

What worked well? Do some children need special attention? How might they be helped? Talk this over with your co-leader. Make a note of any rough spots, problems, or concerns, and consult with one another about how these may be avoided or better handled in future sessions.

What special time are you planning for next Sunday? Have you agreed upon the leaders' major responsibilities? Review the session plan and the Preparation and Materials sections to be sure you have everything you need.

Fill out a weekly leaders' report form according to the custom in your religious education program, being sure to note whatever assistance or special resources you will need.

New Friends and Old

by Mary Ann Moore

Alexandra woke up on Sunday morning and knew that something exciting was going to happen. She couldn't quite remember what it was at first, but when she smelled muffins baking, she said to herself, "It's Sunday and we're going to church. Oh, I hope Emily's there!"

It was the first Sunday after vacation. Alexandra and Emily didn't go to the same school, so they usually saw each other only at church. Once in awhile they played at each other's houses, but not often enough! Alexandra thought about all the fun they had last year—especially making the creche animals and their own "homes" from cardboard boxes in their *Haunting House* class. She jumped out of bed, dressed, and hurried downstairs to gobble up some of those muffins before it was time to go to church.

About the same time, in another part of town, Jason woke up too, but with a funny kind of feeling in his stomach as he *tried* to remember what was going to happen today. It was something he wasn't sure he was going to like. In fact, it was something he didn't think he wanted to do. But what was it? Oh, yes! This morning he and his parents were going to go to that church near the center of town. He had seen the church lots of times when they drove by it, and had always wanted to see what it was like inside. But when his mother told him they were going to go there this Sunday, he wasn't so sure.

He wondered, "What will I have to do there? Who will the other kids be? What if they don't like me? Will I have a friend?"

"Jason, it's time to get ready for church," his mother said when she came to his room. Jason got up, and very slowly, started to get dressed.

When Alexandra got to church she ran inside to see if Emily was there. And she was! They started talking at the same time, jabbering on about the things that had happened to them during the summer. When Jason arrived at the classroom door, with his mother by his side, he looked around, pretending he was interested in how the room looked. Soon his mother left, and Ms. Barton, one of the teachers, invited Jason to join the other children in making name tags. Ms. Barton was friendly, and he liked printing his name carefully and decorating the name tag. He began to feel a little better about being there.

Later there was a time when everyone could choose from several things to do. Alexandra and Emily went over to a table and started making little animals out of clay. Jason stood for a few minutes looking around, trying to decide what to do. He liked to make things out of clay, but he saw the two girls working together and didn't know if they would want him to join them. He edged closer to them.

"Do you want some clay, too?" Alexandra asked, when she saw him looking at their animals.

"Yes," he said. "Are you making animals for the zoo?"

"No, we're making two of each for Noah's Ark!" the girls told him. "Want to help?" And soon they had zebras, elephants, dogs, turkeys, giraffes, and boa constrictors—two of each!

When Jason's parents came to meet him after the church service his mother asked, "How was it, Jason? Did everything go all right?"

"I made two friends," he said. "And we made lots of animals out of clay! Emily and Alexandra told me there's a place where everyone goes after church to have cookies and juice and things. Can we go there?"

In the big room where lots of grown ups and children were talking and eating and drinking coffee or punch, Alexandra found her parents. She told them all about her good morning and how much fun it was to see Emily. "I made a new friend, too," she said. "His name is Jason."

There's No One in the World Like Me

Music: "If You're Happy and You Know It"

There is no one in the world like me.
There is no one in the world like me.
No mat-ter where you go, ov-er land and sea and snow. There's no one in the world like me.

Make New Friends

Words & Music: Traditional Round

Make new friends but keep the old; One is sil-ver and the oth-er gold.

16 Special Times

2 A Time for Worship— Shabbat and Sabbath

Goals for Participants

- To feel a growing sense of self-esteem and belonging to the group.
- To learn of the importance in both Judaism and Christianity of a day of rest and worship.
- To discover the origins of Shabbat/Sabbath as told in the biblical story.

Materials

- Name tags from Session 1 and name tags for newcomers
- A copy of the book, *The Creation,* by Steven Mitchell
- Butcher paper, crayons, markers, and colored pencils
- Materials of your choice for Special Corners
- Chalice, candle, and matches

Preparation

- Read through the session plan and determine who will be responsible for each part of the session.

- Make a sign, "*Special Times* celebrates today *Shabbat/Sabbath,*" for the Unitarian Universalist poster. Hang the poster on the classroom door.

- Gather a selection of books from the Bibliography that are appropriate to the theme of the morning.

- Set up work tables for the mural-making activity and set aside a collection of markers, colored pencils, and crayons. Label sections of the mural paper with the following:

First day	light and darkness/day and night
Second day	sky and earth and seas
Third day	all kinds of plants
Fourth day	sun, moon, and stars
Fifth day	living creatures of sky and seas
Sixth day	living creatures of earth

- Arrange your meeting room similar to the Opening Session with seating in a circle and the four calendars and "About Me" posters on the walls or bulletin boards.

Background

This session engages the children in exploring the roots of the day of worship and rest—Shabbat/Sabbath. The Bible (Genesis 1 and 2) says that God created day and night, earth and sky, the sun, moon and stars, trees and plants, birds and fishes, and all the wild and gentle animals that lived on earth. When all other creations were finished, God created man and woman and called them Adam and Eve. And on the seventh day of creation, God rested from all work, and all that was created rested, too. It was the first Shabbat, the first Sabbath. It was a very peaceful and holy time.

It is likely that the Sabbath was observed before the writing of the Genesis story in sixth century B.C.E. (Before the Common Era). In agricultural societies of that time, the seventh and final day of the week was observed as a day of rest. Since the formulation of the Genesis stories from oral tradition in the fifth century B.C.E., the origin of the Sabbath has been linked with the story of creation in which God rested on the seventh day. The Jewish Shabbat is observed each week on Friday night and all day Saturday—from sunset on Friday until sunset on Saturday. Early Jewish Christians observed the Sabbath on Saturday, but Gentile Christianity gradually shifted the Sabbath to Sunday, honoring the day of Jesus' resurrection.

This concept of the Sabbath is one of Judaism's major contributions to the culture of the western world. Jews remember the Sabbath, and they are obeying the fourth of the Ten Commandments which says, "Six days shall you labor and do all your work. But the seventh day is a Sabbath to the Lord your God. You shall not do any manner of work for the Lord blessed the Sabbath day and hallowed it." This concept is explored more fully in Session 23 on Shavuot.

This session uses the book *The Creation* by Steven Mitchell. Before the session, obtain a copy of it and familiarize yourself with the story.

Session Plan

Gathering   Varies

Greet each child as they arrive and listen to what they may want to share with you. Give them their name tags. Find or make a name tag for each newcomer, and ask her or him to wear it.

Review the four calendars briefly, talking about the special times in each tradition. Add the names and birthdates of newcomers on the Birthday Calendar. Sing the song, "There Is No One in the World Like Me" (see Session 1), alternating the words "me" or "you." Then conclude by singing, "There Is No Group in the World Like Us" or "There Is No Circle in the World Like Ours."

Then say something like, "We usually sit in a circle. Let's play a circle game called 'Around in Circles.' I will call out a description and all of you who fit that description should stand up, turn around and shout 'Around in circles,' and then sit back down. Let's practice. Attention everyone! Stand up. (Pause) Turn around in a circle as you shout 'Around in circles.' (Pause) Sit back down. (Pause) All ready, now let's play." Call out various descriptions, such as all children who:

Have a missing tooth
Have a sister
Have brown hair
Like to eat pizza
Have freckles
Take piano lessons
Play soccer
Like the color purple
Have a pet

For the last description, say, "All children who are great kids in this Unitarian Universalist circle."

Focusing   5 minutes

Ask the children to sit down again in the circle. Then say something like, "This morning we will be celebrating Shabbat/the Sabbath/the special day each week that is set aside for worship and rest. What day of the week is it for you and Unitarian Universalists?" Invite responses.

Then ask, "What makes Sunday morning different from any other day?" Invite their responses which may include statements like not going to school, parents not going to work, or making a special breakfast or dinner.

Then involve the children in a conversation. Say, "Worship means thinking about and celebrating things that are very important. When we worship or celebrate special times, we often do special things and and say special words. Can you tell me some of the things you do or say at home on special celebration days?" Invite responses. Then continue, "What are some special things we do when we worship together as (name of your congregation) Unitarian Universalists?" Invite their responses and comments.

Conversation and Story   15 minutes

Tell the children, "The Sabbath is a very old Jewish celebration. Long, long ago, when the Jewish people worked hard for many hours every day planting in the fields and caring for their farm animals, the seventh day of the week was set aside so they could rest from their work and worship their god. For the Jews, the seventh day was their day of worship and they called it

Shabbat. Do you know what day of the week Jewish people worship?" Pause for answers and comments.

Continue by saying, "Yes, the Jewish Shabbat began at sundown on Friday and ended at sundown on Saturday. Today Jews celebrate Shabbat in many different ways. Some customs include setting the Friday evening Shabbat table in the home with the best dishes, with wine, with sweet braided bread called *challot* and with candlesticks. A blessing, or special words, is spoken to mark this time as holy before the meal is eaten. On Shabbat morning, the family attends services in the synagogue. On Saturday evening a special blessing is said thanking God for the Sabbath and a new week has started.

"But others observe Sunday as their Sabbath, their day to rest and worship their god. Who are these people? What is their religion called?" Pause and invite responses.

Introduce the story, *The Creation*. Say, "Making the seventh day of the week a day of rest and worship comes from an old, old story of how the world was made. We think that when this story says a 'day,' it is really talking about a long period of time—maybe even thousands and thousands of years! This is the story."

Read the story, *The Creation*.

Show the pictures illustrating the text. Intersperse with questions or ask the following questions:

- What things were created first? Last?
- Why do you think things happened in that order?
- Why do you think people were created on the last day?
- Why do you think God rested? Why should people stop work and rest?

If the children seem restless explain the mural-making activity when they will be drawing their own pictures to illustrate the biblical creation story. Read the following poem either before or after reading *The Creation*, whichever is appropriate to focus your group.

And On The Seventh Day . . .
On the first day, God created light and darkness, night and day, the evening and the morning.
On the second day, the Heaven above, and the earth below, the dry land and the seas.
On the third day, all kinds of plants.
On the fourth day, the sun, the moon, and the stars.
On the fifth day, sea monsters and fishes, all the creatures of the water, and winged birds of every kind.
On the sixth day, beasts of the earth, and cattle, and everything that creeps upon the ground. Oh, and people, too.
And on the seventh day, God rested.
Wouldn't you?

Activities 20 minutes

Let the children's imaginations enjoy the story and pictures from *The Creation*, by Steven Mitchell. Clarify any difficult words and ask if they can tell from the story how God felt about creating their world.

Invite the children to make a mural or frieze of the story. Explain that a mural is a big picture with many parts and a frieze is a long picture made up of separate pictures and that their picture will tell a story from beginning to end. Help them decide what kind of picture they want to do as a group and what part of the picture each wants to work on.

Show the mural paper you've prepared and have each of the children choose which day they would like to draw. Move them to the day where it is labeled on the paper.

After the children have completed their drawings, invite them to look at the whole mural or frieze, then print the heading, "Creation," on the mural and hang it on the wall. Gather everyone in front of the mural to "rest" and to affirm the creative efforts of all. Save the mural for displaying to parents in Session 3.

Choices Time Varies

If time permits, invite the children to browse among the Special Corners and look at the books, or play with the puzzles or games. If it is your custom, this could be a time for snacks.

Closing Circle 5 minutes

Gather the children in a circle, light the chalice or candle and say, "With the light of our candles before us, we sit in the quiet and watch the flames. (Pause) Our hearts, hands, and spirits are at rest as we give thanks for this Sabbath day. Amen."

Ask a child to blow out the candle and say good-bye until next Sunday's special time.

Evaluation and Planning

What parts of the sessions went well? Where were there problem areas? How may they be handled differently another time? What needs to be strengthened?

Decide what will be the session topic for next week and make arrangements with one another for planning. What materials or resources will be needed for next week? For the next month of sessions?

If your next class is Session 3, Rosh Hashanah, be sure to review the session thoroughly and remember to mail a letter (see Resource 5) to each participant before the session meets.

3. A Time for the Year to Begin— Rosh Hashanah

Goals for Participants

- To learn that the years go around in cycles and seasons.
- To learn about the autumn celebration of the Jewish New Year.
- To feel the joy of new beginnings and the responsibility of correcting past wrongs.

Materials

- Copies of Resource 5, "Rosh Hashanah Letter to Participants and Parents," for each participant.
- Copies of Resource 6 "Rosh Hashanah Symbols," for each participant.
- Stickers with Rosh Hashanah symbols
- Shofar (ram's horn) or the tape "Sounding of the Shofar" from *Holidays and Holy Days*
- Cassette player (optional)
- Potato stamps with Rosh Hashanah symbols and designs
- Stamps pads or shallow containers of tempera paint
- White drawing paper and colored construction paper
- Scissors
- Markers: blue, green, yellow, and orange
- Apples, an apple slicer or knife, and honey for dipping
- Container and plates
- Challah bread (optional)
- Chalice, candle, and matches
- Books about Jewish holidays and the seasons, such as:
  The Reasons for Seasons: The Great Megagalactic Trip Without Moving From Your Chair, by Linda Allison
  Ring of Earth: A Child's Book of Seasons, by Jane Yolen
  We Celebrate New Year, by Bobbie Kalman and Tina Holdcraft
  A Picture Book of Jewish Holidays, by David A. Adler
  Poems for the Jewish Holidays, selected by Myra C. Livingston

Preparation

- Early in the week, make copies of Resource 5 and mail them before this session meets.

- Read through the entire session plan. Decide who will lead each part of the session.

- Make a sign, "*Special Times* celebrates today *Rosh Hashanah,*" for the Unitarian Universalist poster.

- If possible, obtain a shofar and find someone who knows how to blow it. You can also use "Sounding of the Shofar," a tape from the curriculum *Holidays and Holy Days,* by Brotman-Marshfield if your church has it, and a picture of a shofar.

- Prepare to tell or read the story, "A New Year."

- Learn the song "Shalom" for the Closing activity. Copy the lyrics on newsprint or the chalkboard to help the children learn the words.

- To make potato stamps for the Activity, cut a potato in half. Sketch a design on it and cut around the design with a knife about 1/4" deep. The raised design will pick up the paint.

Session 3: A Time for the Year to Begin 21

- Display the four calendars, the UU poster, the Creation mural from Session 2, and the "About Me" posters on the walls or bulletin boards.

- Gather all necessary supplies and resources for activities and Special Corners.

Background

Rosh Hashanah, the Jewish New Year, marks the beginning of the High Holy Days, a time of meditation and repentance. According to Jewish belief, the first New Year's day was the day God finished the creation of the world. "Rosh" means head and "Hose" means year, literally the "head of the year."

The focal place of Rosh Hashanah is the synagogue rather than the home. The main themes of the services are that God is the creator of the world and God continues to renew creation. In this period of penitence, God is in the process of judging all living things.

Rosh Hashanah as the New Year and Yom Kippur as the Day of Atonement are the first and last days of this ten-day Jewish celebration. This period is devoted to a careful examination of who we are in an attempt to become aware of the ways we have failed—failed others, failed ourselves, failed God. This introspection is meant to lead to regret for the wrongs we have done, to attempts to reconcile our relations with others, and to better ourselves in acting differently in the coming new year.

According to Jewish tradition, there is a symbolic book in heaven in which all of a person's deeds are written. On one side are the good deeds and on the other, the bad deeds. On Rosh Hashanah, Jews believe that God begins a study of each person's behavior for the past year. Has she or he been a good person? Has she or he been hurtful or helpful? God studies all of the person's actions. For the whole ten days the heavenly book is kept open. As the sun goes down on Yom Kippur, God writes down what the person's life will be like for the year to come.

Because a person's fate is not sealed until the end of Yom Kippur, Jews spend time in these ten days of the High Holy Days trying to make themselves better people. They try to repent (to understand the wrongs they may have done in their lives) and then try to change their ways. They hope that by repenting they will be written down for a better life in the coming year. It is a very serious and holy time.

Rosh Hashanah is celebrated by eating a special rounded loaf of challah bread. This reminds people that the year goes around and around. It is also a custom to eat sweet things, such as slices of apple or challah dipped in honey. Honey is the symbol of a sweet year. The traditional new year's greeting is "May you be written down for a good year!"

Session Plan

Gathering   Varies

Greet the children individually as they arrive. Give them some Rosh Hashanah stickers and invite them to decorate the Jewish Calendar and the *Special Times* sign on the Unitarian Universalist poster. Hang the poster on the classroom door.

As the children gather, sound the shofar or play the appropriate segment of the tape "Sounding of the Shofar." Say something like, "Today we're going to talk about change and new beginnings."

Focusing   10 minutes

Say, "Last Sunday we learned that it took millions of years for the earth to form, but how it came to be is still a mystery. But the story of creation in the Hebrew Bible says there is one God who made it possible for the world to be. The story also told us that there is an order to the world."

Look at the mural and invite each child to name the day and part she or he drew. Affirm each child's contribution to the mural.

Then ask, "Is the creation of the world finished?" Talk about the opportunities we have each day to help make the world a better place—work of teachers, scientists, construction workers, doctors, farmers, etc. Ask, "What can children do to make the world a better place?" Talk about some of their accomplishments over the last week, month, or year.

With the children seated in a circle, let them examine the shofar, or show them a picture of one. Ask the children if they know or can guess what the shofar is used for. Add the following to their answers: It is used to call the people to worship or celebrate, to announce the beginning of the High Holy Days, to remind us that God is our creator, and to warn us that we need to change and/or improve.

Conversation and Story   20 minutes

Read the story, "A New Year."

Afterwards, engage the children in a conversation about new years with questions like:

- What kinds of new years can you think of?
- If there are beginnings, what about endings?
- Do things end or do they just change?

Activity   15 minutes

Point out the materials for making Rosh Hashanah cards (Shanah Tovah cards) on work tables, including the potato stamps and the books about the seasons and Jewish holidays in the Reading Corner. After children make their cards, they can help cut apples for the closing circle.

Closing Circle   5 minutes

Place apple slices or challah bread on the table, with honey for dipping.

Light the chalice or candle. Pass around the plate of apples and honey. Invite the children to dip an apple slice in a bit of honey and to eat it.

Then say "This is a special Jewish New Year custom, and it's a way of wishing for a sweet new year. Let's say Happy New Year in Hebrew: Shanah Tovah!"

Read the following poem, "Rosh Ha-Shanah Eve," by Harry Philip:

Stale moon, climb down.
Clear the sky.
Get out of town.
Good-bye.
Fresh moon, arise.
Throw a glow.
Shine a surprise.
Hello.
New Year, amen.
Now we begin:
Teach me to be a new me.

Close by saying, "May each of you be written down for a good year."
Sing "Shalom."

Evaluation and Planning

What went well? Did the children seem to understand the concepts discussed? How can you help to clear up any apparent misunderstandings in future sessions?

If Yom Kippur is to be observed next week, you will need the shofar or tape again.

A New Year

by Mary-Lib Whitney

Timothy and Sarah were all ready for school. They were just finishing their breakfast when Mom walked into the room. "Happy New Year," she said, smiling. She picked up a notebook and began writing in it.

"Happy New Year?" said Sarah. "It won't be the new year for three more months."

"Oh, yes. There are lots of new year days in the calendar," explained Mom. "Some people believed that the new year began in spring when all the new plants began to grow, or in September when they picked all the vegetables and grains. Others think it begins on November first when the earth begins to go to sleep. Can you think of other new years?"

"I guess the day we go back to school at the end of summer, or the day we go back to church are kinds of new years," said Timothy.

Sarah was excited now as she began to think of more. "Our birthdays are all new year days, and in a way, the day Grandma died was a new year day. It was the beginning of a year without her living here. And Christmas might be a new year for Christians because Jesus was born on that day."

"My friend David told me that when he goes to temple on Saturdays, they read from the Torah. When they get to the end and start over again, they have a party. He called that a kind of new year," said Timothy. "Oh, I know! David said he wouldn't be in school today because it was Rosh Hash . . . sh . . . " Timothy stumbled over the word.

"Rosh Hashanah," said Mom, smiling. "That's a big word for a little boy. Yes, you're right. The Jewish people believe that day is the world's birthday. They eat special round loaves of bread to show that the year goes round and round to a new beginning. They also eat apples dipped in honey for a sweet new year."

"Can we do that, Mom?" asked Timothy.

"Sure. I'll make your favorite pizza for supper. That's round like the year, and how about a nice apple pie sweetened with honey?"

"Oh, great," said Sarah. She thought for a minute and then asked her mother, "Why do you keep writing in that notebook?"

"Well, I'm writing down all the things you do, all the bad things and all the good things. I just wrote down how well you thought up ideas about new years."

"Why?" both children asked at the same time.

"The Jewish people believe that God keeps a big book and writes all the things people do. On Rosh Hashanah, God opens the book for everyone to read. They spend a week thinking about the things they have done wrong and try to make them better before God closes the book again. Instead of saying 'Happy New Year,' Jewish people say 'May you be written down for a good year.' I think it would be fun to look at the good things you do as well as the not-so-good things you do. Then, at the end of the week, we can see how well you've done, and how we can help to keep this a happy home."

"We'll have to be really careful how we behave," said Timothy. "Say, this is kind of like being good for Santa."

"Can we write in the book for you and Dad, too?" asked Sarah.

"Sure," said Mom. "I think that's a great idea. And now I think you'd better hurry before I have to write in the book that you missed the school bus."

Shalom Havayreem

Words & Music: Traditional Hebrew Round

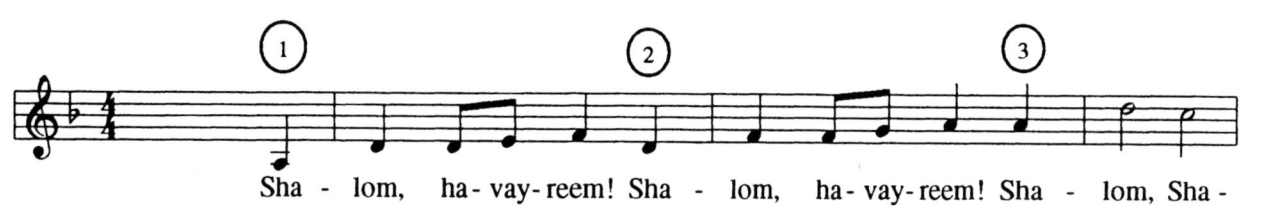

Sha - lom, ha - vay - reem! Sha - lom, ha - vay - reem! Sha - lom, Sha - lom! Sha - lom, ha - vay - reem! Sha - lom, ha - vay - reem! Sha - lom, Sha - lom.

"Shalom, havayreem" means "Peace, friends."

4 A Time for Forgiveness—Yom Kippur

Goals for Participants

- To think about how we know when we've done something wrong.
- To learn that we should say "I'm sorry" and try to make amends for our wrongs.
- To learn that forgiveness is always possible.

Materials

- Stickers of Jewish stars, shofar, books, or whales
- Shofar or the tape, "Sounding of the Shofar," from *Holidays and Holy Days*
- Cassette player (optional)
- Newspaper and paper towels
- Play dough
- Markers, pens, and pencils
- White drawing paper and colored instruction paper
- Chalice, candles, and matches
- Books about Jewish High Holy Days, including those mentioned in the last session. Add *Jonah and the Great Fish*, by Warwick Hutton and *The Book of Jonah*, by Peter Spier

Preparation

- Read through the entire session plan and decide who will lead each part of the session.

- Make a sign, "*Special Times* celebrates *Yom Kippur* today," for the Unitarian Universalist poster.

- Make a Book of Life out of a large blank book. Label the cover "Book of Life." When the book is opened, one side should be labeled "Good Deeds," and the other side labeled "Bad Deeds."

- Make or buy play dough, one can per child.

- Prepare to tell or read the story, "Jonah and the Great Fish."

- Practice singing the song "Shalom" from Session 3. Copy the lyrics on newsprint or the chalkboard to help the children learn the words.

- Obtain and prepare all the necessary materials for activities and Special Corners.

Background

Yom Kippur comes exactly ten days after Rosh Hashanah. It is the holiest day of the Jewish year. On this day, Jews believe that God decides on the kind of life each person will have for the coming year.

God opens a heavenly Book of Life on Rosh Hashanah. For ten days, God studies a person's deeds over the past year. Jews spend these ten days repenting for their sins. They try to understand their behavior and the things they may have done wrong. They try to find ways to make themselves better people. On Yom Kippur, the Day of Forgiveness, a person's future is decided and the Book of Life is closed for another year.

Yom Kippur is a fast day, and Jews eat no food and drink no water for twenty-five hours. They believe fasting helps them to keep their minds clear. Jews spend most of their time of Yom Kippur in the synagogue praying and repenting.

During the Ten Days of Penitence, Jewish

people ask for forgiveness from anyone they may have hurt. They believe that they can ask only God's forgiveness after they have asked others to forgive them, and they try to forgive each other. Yom Kippur gives Jews a chance to right wrongs and make the new year better than the last one.

Session Plan

Gathering   Varies

Greet the children individually as they arrive and give them stickers to decorate the Jewish Calendar and the *Special Times* sign on the Unitarian Universalist poster. Hang the poster on the classroom door.

As the children gather, sound the shofar or play the tape. Gather everyone into a circle on chairs or on a rug. If you have not had the Rosh Hashanah session, explain the origin and significance of the shofar.

Show the children your Book of Life. Remind (or tell) them about the belief that God keeps a book in heaven for each of us, and that it is opened only at Rosh Hashanah and closed after Yom Kippur. Explain that in the days between these two holy days, each person has a chance to say "I'm sorry" and to make up for any wrongs done. Then, it is hoped that one's name will be written down for a good year!

Focusing   10 minutes

Ask the children, "Have you ever made a promise?" Before encouraging them to share some promises they have made, tell them some of your own. Some examples the children may come up with are to be helpful to parents, to share with brothers and sisters, to play fair with friends, to try harder for teachers, and so on.

Then ask, " Do you always keep your promises?" Engage the children in a conversation about how they feel when they don't keep their promises, when they make excuses and have to say "I'm sorry." Remember to include your own difficulties as well.

Continue, "It is hard to ask for forgiveness. It is hard to say 'I'm sorry.' But it is important to say it and mean it. It is even harder to forgive others when they hurt us. On Yom Kippur, Jews have the chance to ask family and friends to forgive themselves and they try to forgive others. The message is that they and we care for and about others, and that they and we want to be friends again."

Conversation and Story   20 minutes

Say something like: "At Yom Kippur, the story of Jonah and the Whale is read in Jewish synagogues and temples—the places where Jews go to worship, like our churches. It is a story about change and forgiveness."

Read the story, "Jonah and the Great Fish."

Afterwards, say something like, "How do we know when we've done something wrong? We don't have to be shipwrecked and swallowed by a whale, do we?" Expect the children to mention instances when their parents or teachers have told them when they've misbehaved; expect some mention of rules and some personal accounts of "being bad."

After a brief discussion of the children's responses, say: "Some people say they hear God talking to them when they've done something wrong; other people say their conscience tells them—a conscience is like a little voice that we hear inside of us. But what's important is that we know when we've done something wrong and feel sorry about it. And it's important to remember that even when we've done something wrong, God, family, and friends all care about and love us."

Activity   10 minutes

Have the children sculpt with the play dough. They can make a whale, hollow out a stomach, and mold a small figure to fit inside.

Choices Time   10 minutes

The children can browse among the books in the Reading Corner, or make another Rosh Hashanah card. It might be fun to have a snack of gold fish cookies.

Closing Circle 5 minutes

Light the chalice and say, "The story of Jonah reminds Jews that God is eager for people to repent—to be sorry for, to feel regret for past wrongs. And if people repent and change, God will forgive and write them down for a good year in the Book of Life."

Close with the children's blessing for Yom Kippur: "May God bless you and protect you. May God's countenance shine upon you. May God be gracious to you, look kindly upon you, and grant you peace."

Sing the song "Shalom."

Evaluation and Planning

What session will be used next week? What preparation do you need for that session?

If your next class is Session 5, Sukkot, read the session thoroughly and remember to mail a letter (see Resource 7) to each participant before the session meets.

Jonah and The Great Fish

Once, a man named Jonah was sitting comfortably in his own land when he heard God speak to him, telling him to go to the city of Nineveh to tell the people there to change their wicked ways and behave in a way pleasing to God. Jonah didn't want to go, because, first of all, he thought the people of Ninevah were bad and deserved to be punished. He knew that if he gave them God's warning, they would beg God to forgive them and God probably would do so. And besides that, he just didn't want to go. So instead, he got on a ship going in the opposite direction.

While he was on the ship, a terrible storm came, and the sailors were very afraid. They threw all their cargo into the sea to make the ship lighter in the water. The storm raged on. The sailors heard the captain ask Jonah to call upon his god to keep them from dying. Then the sailors asked Jonah, "Where do you come from? Why are you here?" When they found out that he was running away from his god, they cried, "This is what you have done! What shall we do to you, that the sea may quiet down?"

Jonah answered, "Pick me up and throw me into the sea, for I know it is because of me that this great storm has come upon you." So they picked him up and threw him into the sea. The sea stopped its raging and the sailors were certain that God had caused the storm.

Jonah was swallowed by a large fish, maybe a whale! He was in the belly of the fish for three nights and three days. He prayed to God to save him. God spoke to the fish, and it tossed him up on dry land. Again, God told Jonah to go to Nineveh, and this time Jonah went and told the people that they would be destroyed if they didn't change their ways. This scared them. They changed their ways, said they were sorry, and begged God to forgive them. And God did, just as Jonah knew God would, and they were not destroyed.

God helped Jonah to understand that although the people of Nineveh had done many bad things, they were good people who were worth saving.

5 A Time for Harvest—Sukkot

Goals for Participants

- To gain greater awareness of the seasons of nature and the time of harvest.
- To build a sukkah and learn about the Festival of Booths.
- To celebrate Sukkot, the Jewish harvest festival of thanksgiving.

Materials

- Copies of Resource 7, "Sukkot Letter to Participants," for each participant.
- Stickers of palm branches, fruits, and vegetables
- Sukkah supplies, such as cornstalks, branches, pine boughs, straw, gourds, flowers, cranberries, popcorn, string, wire, yarn, scissors, large needles
- Harvested vegetables and fruits
- Carrots and apples for snack
- Carrot scraper and apple slicer
- Camera and film
- Chalice, candle, and matches

Preparation

- Read through the entire session plan and decide who will lead each part of the session. Additional adult or parent helpers may need to be recruited to build the structure of the sukkah and to photograph the group.

- Early in the week, make copies of Resource 7 for each participant and mail them before this session meets.

- Make or plan the making of a sukkah, a temporary structure/booth/hut. Traditionally, this is a booth with an open roof covered with palm branches. (See the pictures and commentary in any of the books of Jewish holidays.) Make your sukkah big enough for your group to eat their snack inside. Your church may have a sukkah frame from previous church school programs. You may be able to use a frame from another curriculum, such as the *Haunting House* barn, or even an outdoor jungle gym if the weather permits.

- Make a sign, "*Special Times* celebrates *Sukkot* today," for the Unitarian Universalist poster.

- Bring enough harvested vegetables and fruits in case some of the children forget theirs. Decide on a place to give or send the vegetables and fruits after this session.

- Practice singing the song "Shalom" from Session 3. Copy the words to the song on newsprint or chalkboard to help the children with the lyrics, if necessary.

- Gather all necessary supplies and materials for activities and Special Corners.

Background

Sukkot is a festival with many names and meanings. The holiday is called the Festival of Booths, reminding Jewish people of their history when they wandered in the desert for forty years after the exodus from Egypt. During that sojourn, they lived in temporary booths or sukkot (sukkah—singular; sukkot—plural). Later, when they went far from home to harvest their crops, they built the same kind of temporary booths to shelter themselves from the elements of nature.

Sukkot is also called the Festival of Harvest. When the harvest was completed, they had an eight-day festival. Long ago, Jews from all over the world travelled to Jerusalem and brought their first fruits to the Holy Temple. The journey was a pilgrimage and the travellers, called pilgrims, needed shelter. They built sukkot in courtyards and on rooftops. The streets were decorated and there were parades and dances and feasts.

Even today, Jews build temporary sukkot for this festival, beginning construction right after Yom Kippur. They eat and sometimes sleep in these booths, which are covered only by palm branches, and commemorate the times their forebears spent in the desert and later in the fields. In this session, participants will finish making and decorating their own sukkah, then all will enjoy a harvest celebration.

Note that both this session and the Thanksgiving Day session (Session 10) suggest taking pictures of the children participating in the celebration. Since the Canadian Thanksgiving may fall on an earlier date than Sukkot, or if you decide to use Session 10 before Session 5, pictures of whichever celebration is held first can be brought out for the later one.

Session Plan

Gathering   Varies

Greet the children individually as they arrive and give them stickers to decorate the Jewish Calendar and the *Special Times* sign for the Unitarian Universalist poster. Hang the poster on the classroom door. Draw their attention to the sukkah frame and ask if they can guess what it is and what it's for. Remind them of the letter you sent home mentioning the sukkah.

Focusing   10 minutes

When the group has gathered, invite the children to join you in a circle. Ask the children to bring the food items they brought from home to the circle area. Ask them to share why they brought that particular fruit or vegetable and if they picked it themselves. Talk briefly about the variety of foods in the basket. Ask them to share one thing they especially like about this season of the year. Begin the sharing yourself, then go around the circle.

Conversation and Story   10 minutes

Engage the children in a conversation about the many meanings of the Jewish festival of Sukkot. Say something like, "In many parts of the world, fall is the time when food is harvested or picked. Today, most of the people in our part of the world don't grow or pick their own food. But years ago, almost everyone helped with the important job of getting all the fruits and vegetables in from the fields. In some parts of the world, that's still true today.

"The harvest was always very hard work, and when it was over, the people often celebrated by holding feasts or festivals. This is a story about how the Jewish harvest holiday of Sukkot, sometimes called the Feast of Booths, came to be.

"For 40 years after the Jewish people escaped from slavery in Egypt, they wandered through the desert. They were waiting to receive the Ten Commandments from God and then to be allowed to enter the Promised Land. Since they wandered from place to place, they did not build permanent houses but lived instead in temporary booths or huts. These were called sukkot (singular—sukkah; plural—sukkot). These were easily built and taken down. But they dreamed of a time when they would be free in their own land and could build homes to protect themselves.

"After the Jewish people entered the Promised Land, most of them became farmers. During the time of harvest, they would go to the fields to cut and gather their crops. But because the fields were far away from their homes and villages, they would live in the fields for the entire period of the harvest. To protect themselves from the sun and heat of the day and the cold and wind of the night, the farmers built huts or sukkot.

"When the harvest was finished, the farmers celebrated. It was a time to thank God for the goodness and bounty of the earth. When there was a Temple in Jerusalem, they would bring the first fruits of their harvest to the Holy Temple.

Thousands of Jews came from far and wide to celebrate. The streets were decorated with fruits, branches, and flowers. There were parades and dances and feasts for eight days. They needed a place for shelter and rest, so they built sukkot on rooftops and in courtyards. It was a time to give thanks to God." Invite comments from the children.

Conclude with, "We will finish making our own sukkah this morning. May it remind us of the shelters the Jewish people built in the desert, the harvest huts they built in the fields, and the booths they built in Jerusalem. May it also remind us that not all families live in peace, safety, and comfort. And may we be thankful for the homes we live in."

Activity   15 minutes

Help the children decorate the sukkah, tying the vegetables and fruits around the frame with yarn or fishing wire. For some items you may need to put the food first in a plastic bag. Tie the flowers and bough on the top and sides of your sukkah frame.

Cut paper into strips half an inch wide, eight inches long. Loop them through one another to make a chain, using tape to close each link. Hang the lengths of chain around the sukkah.

Choices Time   Varies

Some children may wish to help prepare the carrots and apples for their snack. Others may wish to continue decorating the sukkah.

Sukkot Celebration   15 minutes

Gather in the sukkah with snack food in the center. Take a picture of the children in the sukkah to use again at Thanksgiving time, or to compare with the picture from the Thanksgiving celebration if it has already taken place. Talk about giving the fruits and vegetables to the shelter or food bank you have chosen.

Sing "Shalom." Then say something like, "We are thankful for all these foods of the harvest, as were the Jews of long ago who began this celebration. Let us eat and enjoy the harvest."

Closing Circle   5 minutes

After the snack and general conversation, light the chalice candle. For closing words say, "We are thankful this day for the fruits of the harvest—the vegetables, grains, and all good foods we grow. May we be ever thankful and always share the food that we have with others. Shalom."

Evaluation and Planning

Where are you sending your fruits and vegetables after this session? Do you want to write a personal note explaining your group and the Sukkot celebration?

How did things go today? What session will be used next week? Are there ways to link upcoming sessions to one another for more continuity? If the Thanksgiving session is still to come, what similarities can we point to for the children?

6 A Time for Learning— Simhat Torah

Goals for Participants

- To experience the joy of the Jewish celebration of Simhat Torah.
- To understand the many meanings of the Torah.
- To learn that the Torah is central to Jewish tradition and is a part of our Unitarian Universalist heritage.

Materials

- Stickers of Torah scrolls, Bibles, and books
- Copies of Resource 8, "Simhat Torah Flag," for each participant
- Shelf paper
- Two rolling pins
- Tape
- Scrap of velvet fabric; velvet ribbon; silver necklace, bracelet, or belt
- Pictures of Torah scrolls from various books on Jewish holidays
- Bible
- Glitter
- White glue
- White cardboard or posterboard
- Dowels (one for each child), 4" wide and 16" long
- Markers, crayons, colored pencils
- Variety of colors of construction paper
- Scissors
- 12 small stones for *Adras* game
- Tape of Jewish dance music
- Cassette player
- Chalice, candle, and matches
- Books with stories celebrated in your church, such as Thanksgiving, Stone Soup, Christmas, Hanukkah, Flower Communion, etc.
- Bible storybooks
- Books used in your religious education program
- Books for the Reading Corner, such as:
  Picture Book of Jewish Holidays, by David Adler
  Poems for Jewish Holidays, by Myra C. Livingston
  Jewish Days and Holidays, by Greer Cashman

Preparation

- Read through the entire session plan and decide who will lead each part of the session.

- Make a "Torah scroll" from shelf paper and two rolling pins. Trim the paper to the width of the rolling pins. Tape each end of the paper securely to one of the rolling pins, so the scroll can be rolled from both ends.
  Inside, print the five books of the Torah—Genesis (Bereshit), Exodus (Shemot), Leviticus (Vayikra), Numbers (Bemidbar), Deuteronomy (Devarim)—and a verse from one of the books of the Torah. Cover it with velvet fabric, trim with something silver, such as costume jewelry, and secure it with velvet ribbon or a silver necklace.

- Make a sign, "*Special Times* today celebrates *Simhat Torah,*" for the Unitarian Universalist poster.

- Find a cassette tape of lively music to dance to, preferably a Jewish song, such as "Hava Nageela," "Dayenu," etc.

- Obtain or prepare the necessary materials and resources for activities and Special Corners.

Background

Each synagogue has its own hand-lettered scrolls of the Torah, the first five books of the Hebrew Scriptures (Old Testament). During a year of weekly services the entire Torah is read, and on Simhat Torah—the Festival of Rejoicing in the Law—the final book is completed and the cycle begins again.

On Simhat Torah, the Torah scrolls are dressed in velvet and silver and jewels. After the final portion is read and prayers are said, the congregation dances jubilantly in circles, singing and passing the Torah scrolls to one another. Children join in the procession, often carrying miniature scrolls and waving flags of many colors and designs.

At the end of the celebration, the Torah scrolls are turned back to the beginning to be read again. Jews believe that there is really no end to the teaching and learning of the Torah and that something new is discovered from each reading.

As we look at the Jewish festival cycle, it seems that Simhat Torah and Shavuot are alike. In certain ways Shavuot (one-day festival) is the conclusion to Pesah (seven-day festival of Passover), just as Simhat Torah (one-day festival) is the conclusion to Sukkot (seven-day festival of harvest). Both began with agricultural and temple rituals. Shavuot became an historical festival commemorating the revelation of God's Law at Sinai. Simhat Torah became a festival based on the synagogue liturgy, the completion of the reading of the whole Torah. But both holidays celebrate the Torah, a rejoicing in the experience of the Divine.

Session Plan

Gathering　　　　　　　　　　　Varies

Have the tape of Jewish dance music playing as the children come in. Greet the children individually as they arrive and give them stickers to decorate the Jewish Calendar and the *Special Times* sign for the poster. Hang the poster on the classroom door. Invite them to look at the display of pictures of Torah scrolls and ask if they know about the Torah and/or the Bible.

Focusing　　　　　　　　　　　10 minutes

Gather the children in a circle and show them the decorated Torah scroll and the Bible.

Say, "A scroll is like a book that you can roll up. Every Jewish synagogue and temple has special scrolls, called the Torah, which look something like this. The 5 books of the Torah are in the Hebrew Bible, and they are in that part of the Christian Bible called the Hebrew Scriptures, or the Old Testament. Can anyone guess why this Torah scroll is decorated with velvet and silver?"

Engage the children in a conversation about the central place of the Torah in the Jewish faith.

Conversation and Story　　　　10 minutes

Lead into the story by saying, "'Torah' has many meanings—Torah as book and scroll, Torah as teaching, Torah as Jewish history and tradition. The Torah is five books in one. It is called the Five Books of Moses, because the Jewish people believe that Moses received the Torah on Mount Sinai." Show them again the names of the five books of the Torah—Genesis, Exodus, Leviticus, Numbers, Deuteronomy—written on the scroll.

"Torah means teaching. The Jewish people believe that the Torah teaches through stories, songs, and poems. They gather in synagogues on Shabbat and special times and holidays, and read from the Torah. Rabbis (clergy) and teachers read a section of the Torah each week and help their people understand how the teachings of the Torah are important guides in leading lives of peace and kindness.

"It takes exactly one year to read the whole Torah. On Simhat Torah the final part is read and then they start all over again from the beginning. They believe there is never an end to learning and that they discover something new each time they read the Torah.

"Besides coming to worship services, celebrations, pot-luck suppers, and meetings, we have a special time here just for learning. Do you know what we call that?" Invite their responses and talk about religious education in your congregation.

Then say, "This is a special time when older

people help younger people, like you, talk about the things we wonder about, things that we believe are important. And teachers, too, learn a lot when they are teaching! We think it's important for grownups, too, to have special times together to keep on learning. We are learning all during our lives, no matter how old we become. What are some of the things we do here to help us learn and grow together?" Allow time for responses.

Continue by saying, "Torah is an important part of the Jewish history and tradition. Simhat Torah celebrates learning and is one of the gayest Jewish holidays. On Simhat Torah morning in some synagogues members of the congregation take turns being the rabbi. After the final section of the Torah has been read, the congregation proclaims 'May our strength increase.' Then the people take the scrolls in their arms and dance in circles around the synagogue. Children join in carrying flags of many colors and designs. There is a lot of singing and dancing and snacks for all. Before the end of the holiday, the Torah scrolls are turned back to the beginning, all set to read again."

If appropriate, close with, "Like reading the Torah over and over every year, we keep on learning more and more every year!"

Activity   15 minutes

Tell the children that they will make flags and end today's session by dancing around with the flags just as the Jewish people do when they celebrate Simhat Torah. Put out materials for making the flags and assist the children as necessary in making them.

Torah Flags

To make the Torah flag, cut out the flag pattern on Resource 8. Trace the pattern on white cardboard and cut out the flag. Cut out the design symbols, trace them on colored paper or fabric, and glue the cut outs to the flag. Or draw and color a design in the center of the flag, such as a small Torah scroll, a six-pointed star, or something of your choosing. Encourage each child to decorate their flag according to their creative insights. Attach the flag to the dowel with tape.

Choices Time   10 minutes

Put on the Jewish dance music again. Point out the stories and books in the Reading Corner, or suggest playing a game of *Adras* (Israeli Tic-Tac-Toe). If it's your custom, have a snack.

Adras

This game requires two players, each with three stones. Players draw a diagram like this one:

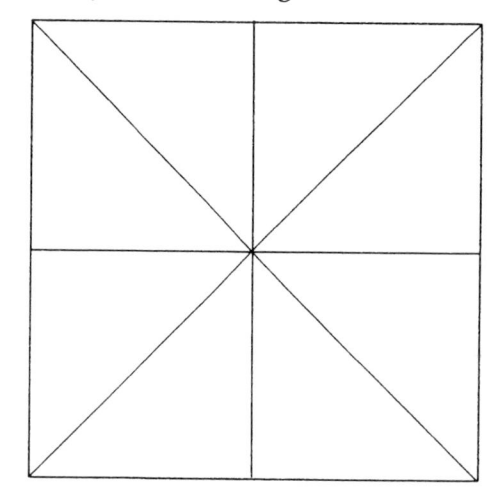

Players take turns placing their stones on the intersections—one stone per move. The winner is the first player to get three stones in a line at intersections in any direction.

Closing Circle   10 minutes

Dance around the room to lively music with an adult carrying the large scroll and the children waving their flags.

Gather everyone in a circle, light the chalice candle, and close by saying, "Let us rejoice in learning and may we keep on learning year after year. Shalom."

Evaluation and Planning

What went well today? Was too much planned? Too little?

What session will be used next week? Are there ways you can plan on-going projects which connect sessions according to your calendar?

7 A Time for Heroes and Heroines—All Saints' Day

Goals for Participants

- To become more familiar with the idea of a "saint."
- To learn about some of the deeds of the Christian saints.
- To appreciate more fully the qualities of living we consider important.

Materials

- Stickers of saints and symbols for the saints, such as shamrocks for St. Patrick, a bird for St. Francis of Assisi, and a Christmas tree for Saint Nicholas
- Information about saint names in your area with which children may be familiar: names of cities, nearby streets, hospitals, Unitarian Universalist churches named in memory of ministers and/or founders, etc.
- Felt rectangles (approximately 9 x 12"), one for each child, in a variety of colors.
- Dowels, 1/8" or 1/4" wide, and 9 1/2" long
- Large and small pieces of felt in a variety of colors
- Scissors
- Paper, cardboard, pens and pencils for making patterns
- White glue
- Tongue depressors (or other holder for carrying banners)
- Yarn to trim ends of dowels for banners (optional)
- Variety of materials in the Craft Center for making hats, headdresses, crowns, crosses to wear on chains, or masks for the saints
- Chalice, candle, and matches
- Tape of "Oh, When the Saints" (optional)
- Cassette player (optional)
- Various Christmas books on Saints Lucia, Nicholas, Stephen, and Wenceslaus, and Unitarian Universalist books, such as:
  People Like Us, by Elizabeth Gillis
  A Stream of Living Souls, by Denise Tracy
  Saints, Signs, and Symbols, by W. Ellwood Post (for symbols of different saints).
- Books for the Book Corner:
  Book of Holidays Around the World, by Alice van Straalen
  The Children's Book of Saints, by Louis M. Savary
  Francis, the Poor Man of Assisi, by Tomie de Paola
  Jeanne d'Arc, by Aileen Fisher, illustrated by Ati Forberg
  Patrick of Ireland, by Wilma Pitchford Hays

Preparation

- Read through the entire session plan and decide who will lead each part of the session.

- Make a sign, "*Special Times* celebrates today All Saints' Day" for the Unitarian Universalist poster.

- Read through the stories of Unitarian Universalist "saints" at the end of this session. Choose the ones you will use for the Conversation and Story activity, or read your own from other books. If you like, invite a Unitarian Universalist guest, such as your minister, religious education coordinator, or lay leader to tell a story about their UU heroes and heroines.

- Plan the processional, if you decide to have one during Choices Time. This might involve a march through the religious education space, into the coffee hour, or just around the classroom. Whatever you decide, coordinate with everyone who will be affected.

- List on newsprint or chalkboard the names of saints the children may have heard about (e.g., Nicholas, Joan of Arc, Francis, Christopher).

- Obtain pictures and/or posters (broadsides) of famous Unitarian Universalists.

- To make banners for the Activity, stitch 9 x 12" felt rectangles across one end to form a flap through which a dowel can be inserted. Leave a space unstitched at the center, just large enough to insert the end of a tongue depressor or other banner holder. Make enough banners for each child.

- Cut a few symbols or designs out of felt to represent each of the saints on your list for this session.

- Obtain all necessary materials and resources for activities and Special Corners.

Background

Dictionaries and encyclopedias define a "saint" in several ways: an official Christian saint, canonized by the Roman Catholic Church; a person who displays to an extraordinary degree the qualities of holiness and goodness; and the members of certain religious groups who have so designated themselves (the Puritans, for example, and the Mormons, who are officially known as "The Church of Jesus Christ of the Latter Day Saints").

Roman Catholics observe the days for all the saints in their liturgical calendar. All Saints' Day was established to honor those martyrs who were unknown and thus had no feast days of their own. Anglicans also observe All Saints' Day, often with a Great Procession of Saints in the service. Protestants have traditionally not included All Saints' Day in their calendar. The "communion of saints" is referred to in the Apostle's Creed in some Christian churches. Although All Saints' Day is a Christian festival, and the resources listed here deal with Christian saints, the eastern religions also honor saints.

Unitarian Universalists honor a wide variety of people who have exhibited "qualities of goodness." There may be Unitarian Universalist heroes and heroines important to your congregation, such as founders or ministers.

This session includes short stories of Samuel Joseph May, Elizabeth Blackwell, Whitney Young, and Amos Peck Seaman as samples of Unitarian Universalist "saints." Stories of your local Unitarian Universalist heroes and heroines also would be important to tell. Stories need to be told in language appropriate to first and second graders with emphasis on the qualities of "goodness" as identified in our Principles and Purposes.

Session Plan

Gathering   Varies

Greet each child individually. Show them the stickers of saints and their symbols. Ask the children if they recognize the saints in the pictures, or if they can think of a saint connected with the symbols. Ask if they know of any other saints. Invite them to decorate the Christian Calendar and the *Special Times* sign with stickers and hang the poster on the door.

Focusing   5 minutes

Gather the children in a circle on chairs or on a rug. Say something like, "We will talk about some of the saints you know about. (Refer to saints mentioned during Gathering.) A saint is someone who is especially good or holy. What kinds of things do people do that show they are truly good, or holy?" Allow time for responses. Encourage them to name Unitarian Universalists who they think are good, and ask them to name people they have heard about who do especially good things.

Conversation and Story — 20 minutes

After the children have thought about saints, say, "Here are some stories about Unitarian Universalist 'saints.'"

Read your choice of the stories, "Samuel May," "Eizabeth Blackwell," "Whitney Young," or "Amos Seaman."

Activity — 20 minutes

Ask the children to name a few people they can think of who do especially good things. After they have named some, ask "What kind of sign or picture might stand for the things your special person does." Allow time for responses. You may need to mention examples, such as birds as the symbol for St. Francis, or a heart symbol for Saint Valentine, or a golf club or knitting needles for their grandfather/grandmother.

Banners for the Saints

Tell the children that they will be making banners to honor the people they have chosen for the special things they do.

Invite each child to choose one of the 9 x 12" felt rectangles you stitched across one end.

On another piece of felt, have them draw and cut out designs or patterns to symbolize the person they have chosen to honor, then glue it onto their banner. (They could also draw the pattern directly onto the banner.) Be sure they position the design so that the stitching runs along the top of the banner.

Insert a dowel through the stitched top. Put glue on the end of a tongue depressor (banner holder) and insert it into the center hole, under the dowel. Press to get the glue to hold. Yarn may be used to trim the ends of the dowels.

Show the children how to hold the banner by the holder, out in front of the body but not covering their faces.

Choices Time — Varies

As the children are finishing their banners, direct them to the available resources, books, and craft materials. Or, you may want to eliminate Choices Time, allowing the children more time for the saints' march.

For the march, play the tape of "Oh, When the Saints," and parade around the classroom or religious education space with the children carrying their banners. If appropriate, and previously arranged, have the children march into other classrooms.

Closing Circle — 5 minutes

Gather the children in a circle. As you light the chalice, say something like, "We light our candle to honor all the saints, both gone before and now living. May we live lives of kindness and fairness, and show our caring for others each day."

Evaluation and Planning

Did the children seem to understand the concepts of sainthood and the qualities which we hold important? Is follow-up needed?

If the children did not take their banners home, arrange a wall display in your classroom or on a hall bulletin board.

If your next class is Session 8, St. Francis' Day, read through the entire session and remember to mail a letter (see Resource 9) to each participant before the session meets.

Samuel Joseph May (1797-1871)

by Patricia Hoertdoerfer

"What crime have these men committed?" Samuel May asked the other stagecoach passengers as he looked out on 30 black men, who were handcuffed and fastened along a heavy chain that was attached to a wagon.

The man next to May turned and said, "They are only slaves some planter has purchased and he's taking them home."

May thought about his situation and said, "I never fully realized before how great a privilege it is to live where human beings cannot be treated in this manner!"

Samuel May was hardly ever away from his hometown of Boston, but when he took this trip South, it changed his life. He decided to dedicate his life to helping people gain their human rights. He studied and became a Unitarian minister, preaching the message of love toward all people. His religion was practical and active, making him work everyday to relieve the suffering and to free the oppressed. What concerned him most was the loss of human rights. He spoke out against slavery and demanded freedom for black people.

May led Unitarians and people from Syracuse, New York, to help black people reach freedom. They helped slaves escape from the southern part of the United States where people were allowed to own slaves and head north to Canada where slavery was forbidden. Samuel May's home became a stop for many slaves along the road to freedom. The act of helping slaves escape to the North was called the Underground Railroad, and May was a good conductor on the Underground Railroad.

Samuel May worked most of his life to rid our country of its worst form of human oppression—slavery. It was not an easy goal for him, and it sometimes meant violent struggle to reach freedom. As he said, "May the sad experience of the past prompt and impel us to do all that righteousness demands at our hands—all that righteousness demands at our hands."

Today people are still suffering and many black people are not treated equally. Yet many liberties have been gained and many people have been helped because of people like Samuel May and other Unitarian leaders who acted with dedication and courage.

Elizabeth Blackwell (1821-1910)

by Elizabeth Gillis

"Elizabeth, it's of no use trying. Thee cannot gain admission to these schools. Thee must go to Paris and don masculine attire to gain the necessary knowledge."

That is what Elizabeth Blackwell was told by a Quaker friend who tried to help her get into medical school. It was in the 1840s and young ladies did *not* go to medical school!

But Elizabeth did not go to Paris or dress up like a man. She thought she had the right to study medicine like any man. She applied to many schools and was rejected by all of them. Finally, she was accepted by a medical school in Geneva, New York. The faculty had presented her request to the students. If one student failed to agree, they said, she would not be admitted. They thought it was a great joke and voted to have her enter the medical school.

She completed her studies and graduated. Elizabeth described her graduation day:

"After the degree had been conferred on the others, I was called up alone to the platform. The president, in full academic costume, rose as I came on the stage and going through the usual formula of a short Latin address, presented my diploma. I said, 'Sir, I thank you; it shall be the effort of my life, with the help of the Most High, to shed honour on my diploma.' The graduates applauded. As I came down, I was much touched by the graduates making room for me, and insisting that I should sit with them for the remainder of the exercises."

What had begun as a joke to many ended in

respect for the young woman who was so determined to be a doctor. However, the medical school was censured for doing such a daring thing.

Dr. Blackwell, a Unitarian for much of her life, had a long career after becoming the first American woman to obtain a degree in medicine.

Whitney Young (1921-1971)

by Denise Tracy

"Where are you going?" his mother asked.

"I'm running away," said the child.

"Where will you go?"

The boy was silent. His suitcase was half full. He had put in some clothes. Now he was putting in the important stuff. His favorite books and a toy or two. He was leaving a lot behind. But where he was going he wouldn't need much. You see, he was going to start a new world where everything was fair and equal.

"Where will you go?" asked his mother again.

"Somewhere where the color of my skin won't matter!" replied the boy with a quiver in his voice.

"What happened?" the mother asked quietly.

"I was walking down the street and two white boys called me a 'nigger.' Then they made me get off the sidewalk so they could pass. I hate them." By now he was crying. "I wish I had never been born and I wish I had never been born black."

"Whitney, your color is beautiful. It's just that some people don't see it that way. Do you know that when I was your age I wanted to run away from home thinking I could find a place where the color of my skin wouldn't matter?"

"You did?" The boy was surprised by how well his mother knew him. Sometimes he thought she could even read his mind.

"Yes, I did. I thought I'd go start all over again in a new place."

"What happened?" asked Whitney.

"Well, my momma saw me packing my bag and said she'd tried to run away and that her momma had caught her and her momma'd remembered the time she'd packed her suitcase, too. All of us have had decisions to make about how to deal with the unfairness of the world."

"Why did you and your momma and your momma's momma decide not to go?"

"Well, my momma's momma told her and momma told me and now I'm telling you, we Youngs don't run from evil, we face it unafraid, and we change it."

"How do you change evil?"

"Well, your momma's momma, my momma, and me all understood that if you believe what some whites want you to—that our color is the problem—then hatred grows. It festers inside you and you grow up bitter. Your momma's momma, my momma, and me all give you a heritage of pride. Those boys on the street feel small inside—that's why they pick on you so they will feel bigger. If you know that their behavior comes from their own ignorance and smallness nothing they can say can hurt you. But let me tell you something else. For three generations our family has been watching the world change and we've been helping it along. It's your turn to change evil."

"But what do I do?"

"You'll know when the time comes."

Whitney Young began to unpack his bag. He'd live in this world and he'd change evil. He came from a long line of people who chose not to run away, not to hate but to change. He felt proud.

When Whitney Young grew up he became the dean of a small college and the director of the National Urban League. As the director of the National Urban League, he allied himself with other black and white people who believed in equality. He started job programs to deal with the evil of unemployment. He wrote grants to train black people to be executives. He founded schools to help black youths who had dropped out of school to get their diplomas so they could find good jobs.

Whitney Young was a Unitarian Universalist. He worked at changing evil wherever he saw it—not by hating it, but by tackling it, understanding it, and changing it.

Amos Peck Seaman (1788-1864)

by Mary Hamilton

Amos Peck Seaman was called the "King" of Minudie, Nova Scotia, in Canada. From very humble beginnings he became a successful business man and generous Universalist leader.

Amos was born in a tiny hut in the small parish of Sackville in eastern Canada on a very cold January day. As Amos grew, he spent many evenings sitting beside his mother as she darned and re-darned their few clothes. Here he learned to read from the Bible, and to count sticks of wood for the fire. In later years, as he sat each evening to write in his daily journal, he would remember quiet hours with his mother.

By the time he was 8, Amos knew he must leave his parents' home. He was an extra mouth to feed and there was nothing he could do in Sackville to bring extra food into the home. He found an old birch bark canoe, and he crossed the Bay of Fundy, arriving in Minudie, Nova Scotia, with no shoes on his feet and only the clothes on his back.

Perhaps it was his name that led Amos Seaman to the sea. He spent these early years working around the docks and shipyards and out sailing on the many ships. By the time he was 22 he was, indeed, a man of the sea. With his brother Job as a business partner, he began trading with the Boston merchants, and soon he was carrying goods between Nova Scotia, New England, and the West Indies in ships built in his own shipyards.

On May 12, 1814, Amos Seaman and Jane Metcalfe were married. With Jane's help, Amos was able to attend school to further his education.

Amos seemed to have a magic touch. He succeeded with whatever business he tried. In 1834 he purchased the 7,000 acre Minudie estate. He gradually enlarged it, even reclaiming some land from the sea, until it was the largest estate in Nova Scotia. The many sandstone deposits on the estate were excellent for the production of grindstones. Soon, thousands of high-priced grindstones were being shipped to American markets.

There was little in the town of Minudie that wasn't touched by Amos Seaman. His businesses included the first steam-powered grist mill, a steam saw-mill, and a coal mine. Along with all of this, he kept a fatherly eye on the people of Minudie, doing what he could to improve their lives. Of course, he liked to have things done his way, and soon became known as "King" of Minudie.

Because he never had an education until he grew up, he knew how important it was for his 11 children (seven boys and four girls) and their friends to go to school, even if they thought it might be more fun to play! He gave the town the lumber to build a fine schoolhouse.

On one side of the school, he built a very special church. He was a Universalist, and he believed that everyone could come and worship in his church, even if they didn't believe as he did. Some of the people were happy to join him, but many of the others weren't happy there. When he learned this, he made the town another gift—a Catholic church which was built on the other side of the school house.

Amos "King" Seaman lived a long time ago, but all three of the buildings—the school, the Universalist church, and the Catholic church—still stand today in Minudie, Nova Scotia. Amos Seaman was an important Universalist leader who believed that every person has the right to worship as she or he sees fit.

8 A Time to Bless the Animals— St. Francis Day

Goals for Participants

- To learn the story of St. Francis of Assisi, who was a friend not only to the poor but also to birds and animals.
- To recognize a kinship to and responsibility for other creatures of the earth.
- To gain an appreciation of our Unitarian Universalist principle of "the interdependent web of all existence."

Materials

- Copies of Resource 9, "St. Francis Day Letter to Participants," for each participant
- Stickers of birds and animals
- Newsprint or posterboard
- Pictures of endangered species and pets or stuffed animals brought in by the children
- Pine cones
- Yarn or string
- Peanut butter or shortening
- Birdseed
- Waxed paper or plastic sandwich bags
- Newspaper
- Plastic spoons
- Paper, scissors, markers, glue, etc., in Craft Center for making animals
- Clay or play dough for modeling animals
- Chalice, candle, and matches
- Books with pictures of birds and animals and the sun, moon, and stars. Books about St. Francis and other saints, such as:
  Francis, the Poor Man of Assisi, by Tomie de Paola
  The Children's Book of Saints, by Louis M. Savary

Preparation

- Read through the entire session plan and decide which activities to include and who will lead them.

- Early in the week, make copies of Resource 9 for each participant and mail them before this session meets.

- Make a sign, "*Special Times* celebrates today *St. Francis Day*" for the Unitarian Universalist poster.

- Gather pictures of endangered species in case the children don't bring any.

- Print in large letters on newsprint, chalkboard, or posterboard: "Unitarian Universalists respect the interdependent web of all existence." Draw a web with various living things on it.

- Decide on any refreshments (perhaps animal crackers).

- Obtain all materials and resources for activities and Special Corners.

Background

The ceremony of the Blessing of the Animals to honor St. Francis of Assisi may take place at any time of the year. In October in New York City, hundreds of people bring their pets to the Cathedral of St. John the Divine to be blessed and to celebrate St. Francis's birthday. In Northern Mexico, children honor St. Anthony, the patron saint of animals, in January. They dress up livestock and pets, paint polka dots and stripes on them, and lead them to the local churchyard for a blessing with holy water by a priest.

Many churches honor St. Francis of Assisi with a blessing of animals. Many issues related to animal rights can be explored through such a celebration. But the focus of this session is on pets and the responsibility of caring for them and living creatures which share our environment.

This session plan is fluid; much will depend on your local setting and the resources you have available. The occasion can be either quite simple or quite elaborate, but above all, it should be festive and fun.

Session Plan

Gathering   Varies

As the children arrive, welcome them and give them the stickers of birds and animals. Invite them to decorate the Christian Calendar and the *Special Times* sign on the poster and hang the poster on the classroom door. Look at the photographs and stuffed animals brought in by the children, and place them where they can be seen for the Closing Circle.

Focusing   5 minutes

Gather everyone in a circle. Ask the children to listen as they each take turns talking about the photograph or stuffed animal they brought. Allow time for responses.

Conversation and Story   20 minutes

Introduce the story as one about a man named Francis who loved animals.

Read the story, "St. Francis of Assisi."

After the story, say, "During activity time, we will make bird feeders to honor St. Francis. But first let's talk about other species—those we call endangered species. What does 'endangered species' mean?" Invite responses.

Invite each child who brought a picture of an endangered species to talk about that particular species. If none of them brought a picture, show ones that you've collected. Conclude your discussion with a focus on the interdependent web drawing and emphasize how all of us need each other to survive and live.

Activity   15 minutes

To make bird feeders, you will need pine cones with a cord tied around the top for hanging, shortening or peanut butter, and bird seed. Use a spoon to spread the shortening or peanut butter on the pine cones and then roll the cones in bird seed. Wrap the cones in waxed paper or put them in plastic sandwich bags to take home.

Choices Time   10 minutes

Point out available choices: the Reading Corner and materials in the Craft Center for drawing pets and for making animals from clay or play dough. This may also be a time for any snack, such as animal crackers, you have planned.

Closing Circle   5 minutes

Light the chalice and invite the children to hold their pet pictures or stuffed animals. Then say something like, "We light this candle for our pets, and for all animals, birds, fishes, plants, flowers, and other living creatures who share this earth with us. Let's all say this Animal Blessing. Repeat the words after me:

"We bless these beasts
   WE BLESS THESE BEASTS
We give them care
   WE GIVE THEM CARE
We care for animals, birds, and fishes
   WE CARE FOR ANIMALS, BIRDS, AND FISHES
Here in our room
   HERE IN OUR ROOM
And everywhere
   AND EVERYWHERE."

Help each child find her or his photograph or stuffed animal and bird feeder to take home. As they leave, affirm each of them as caregivers to their pets and to our earth's birds and beautiful living things.

Evaluation and Planning

How did things work? Who should be thanked for helping? What recommendations would you make for this session another year?

Do you want to follow up on endangered species information or action in your local area?

If your next class is Session 9, All Souls' Day, read through the entire session and remember to mail a letter (see Resource 10) to each participant before the session meets.

St. Francis of Assisi

Francis was born a long time ago in 1182 in Italy, in the town of Assisi. Although his family was rich, years later the story was told that he had been born in a stable behind the family home! (Ask, "What other story do we know where someone was born in a stable?" Invite responses.)

When Francis grew up, he shared what he had with the church and with the poor. He also gave away things and money which belonged to his father. His father tried to stop this behavior. When the judge would do nothing, he took Francis before the Bishop of the church, who said that Francis should not give away his father's goods, but only his own.

When the Bishop told Francis to give his father's money back, Francis did more than that. He took off his own fine clothes and gave them to his father, too! After that Francis wore the clothing of a peasant or farmer.

Francis started a group called a brotherhood with other men who wanted to serve God and the poor. Francis and the other members of this brotherhood promised to live like the poor people. They called their brotherhood the Friars Minor, which means "the littlest brothers."

After some time with the brotherhood, Francis decided that he wanted to go off to live completely alone. But his friends convinced him that God wanted him to preach and to teach others.

Francis first preached to the birds! (Ask, "Do you know the special name we have for this kind of person?" Invite responses. Then show the pictures in the de Paola book.) Later, he is said to have tamed a wolf! Francis believed that people, animals, birds, and the sun and the moon and the stars were all related and connected.

In 1228, the Roman Catholic Church declared Francis a saint, a person who is especially good and holy. Francis's special feast day is October 4.

9 A Time to Remember Those Who Have Died—All Souls' Day

Goals for Participants

- To learn that all people lose loved ones to death.
- To explore the concept that although death is natural and inevitable, so too is grief.
- To share and honor memories of those who have died.

Materials

- Copies of Resource 10, "All Souls' Day Letter to Parents and Participants," for each participant
- A copy of the book, *The Great Change*, by White Deer of Autumn, or *Lifetimes: The Beautiful Way to Explain Death to Children*, by Byron Mellonie and Robert Ingpen
- Flowers or a beautiful object, such as a stone, shell, or pine cone to be used as a centerpiece
- Stickers of flowers and shells
- Clay or play dough
- Finger paints
- Blank sheets of paper with "I Remember" printed on top
- Candles (one for each person) and a dish or tray with sand
- Chalice, candles, and matches
- The following books for the Reading Corner. Include books with pictures of cemetaries and gravestones (even if the text is intended for adults).
  The Dead Bird, by Margaret Wise Brown
  How It Feels When a Parent Dies, by Jill Krementz
  Ira Says Good-bye, by Bernard Waber
  My Grandpa Died Today, by Joan Fassler
  My Grandson Lew, by Charlotte Zolotow
  Nana Upstairs, Nana Downstairs, by Tomie de Paola
  The Tenth Good Thing About Barney, by Judith Viorst
  What We Do When Someone Dies, by Caroline Arnold
  It Must Hurt a Lot: A Child's Book about Death, by Doris Sanford
  Explaining Death to Children, by Earl A. Grollman

Preparation

- Read through the entire session plan and decide who will lead each activity.

- Early in the week, make copies of Resource 10 for each participant and mail them before this session meets.

- If your society has a memorial garden, memorial windows, memorial walk, or a cemetery, plan to share them with the children. Invite the minister, religious education coordinator, or lay leader to tell the class about your society's memorial garden or room.

- Make a sign, "*Special Times* celebrates today *All Souls' Day*" for the Unitarian Universalist poster.

- Read or tell the story *Lifetimes: The Beautiful Way to Explain Death to Children*, by Bryan Mellonie and Robert Ingpen, or *The Great Change*, by White Deer of Autumn. Share the beautiful drawings and illustrations in the books with the children. The Closing Circle is similar to the candle activity in the UUA curriculum, *A Haunting House*. Become familiar with the story you choose to read or tell, as well as the closing activity, so that you can pay attention to the children's feelings and sharings during the session.

- Practice singing "We Each Have Our Precious Memories" for the Song activity and prepare to teach it to the children, or arrange for a music assistant to do this. Copy the lyrics on newsprint or the chalkboard to help the children with the words.

- Obtain all necessary materials and resources for activities and Special Corners.

Background

Many of the children will have experienced the death of pets. Some will have had more painful experiences, such as the loss of a grandparent or other relative, perhaps a friend or even a parent or sibling. It will be helpful for you to be aware of such losses, so be sure to send out the letter to participants and parents early in the week.

Obviously, one sixty-minute session is not long enough for an in-depth study of death. The focus here is more limited, to the idea of remembering and honoring those who have died. This is the purpose of the Christian festival of All Souls. Include in your discussion the names of Unitarian Universalist or Christian All Souls churches in your area.

As far back as we can go, people have marked the graves of their loved ones. The first stones placed on graves were no doubt to prevent animals from digging them up, but they soon became markers. Many pre-historic people are said to have placed flowers on graves. Death remains a very special mystery for all people and for all religions, and all religions have developed special ceremonies to help us cope with death.

Session Plan

Gathering   Varies

As the children arrive, hand out stickers and ask them to decorate the Christian (and UU) Calendars and the *Special Times* sign on the poster. Hang the poster on the classroom door. The children will probably want to show you the pictures they brought and tell you and the other children about them.

Focusing   10 minutes

Gather in a circle on chairs or on a rug, with flowers or a large, beautiful object in the center. Invite each child to tell about the person in their photographs and then place them by the centerpiece. Leaders can participate in this, too.

Conversation and Story   15-20 minutes

Say something like, "All of us know about someone who has died, don't we? How does that make us feel?" Allow time for responses.

Then, depending on your own circumstances, say something like, "It makes me feel sad when someone I care about dies. I feel the same way—only not as strongly—when someone I know about from the news dies, like (name a public figure who has recently died). And when my pet (dog/cat) died, I felt just awful.

"Even a long time afterward, I still feel sad sometimes about (mention a specific death).

"But even after a person has died, we remember that person, don't we? Each of you told us something about the person (or pet) whose picture you brought. Now we have something about that person in our memories, too!

"People in some Christian churches remember and honor on November 2 their loved ones who have died. On that day, which they call All Souls' Day, they light a candle or bring flowers to put on the grave in the cemetery. But most of all, they remember that person.

"Let me read you a story about life and death."

Read the story, *The Great Change* or *Lifetimes*.

Allow time for comments from the children after you have read the story.

Song   5 minutes

Sing "We Each Have Our Precious Memories." Stand in a circle, or walk or dance gently around in a circle as you sing.

Alternate Activity   15 minutes

Walk around the memorial garden or memorial room. Invite the minister, religious education coordinator, or lay leader to explain why your congregation has such a memorial.

Choices Time   20 minutes

Point out the Reading Corner and the items available in the Craft Center: clay or play dough, finger paints. Say something like, "You may want to write or draw something you remember about someone who died. Or with finger paints, show how you feel when you remember a person, or a pet, who died."

Closing Circle   10 minutes

Gather in a circle and light the chalice. Place candles in a tray or dish of sand in the center of the circle. Light a taper from the chalice candle and use it to light another candle. Say, "I light this candle for (name of a person who has died)."

Pass the taper around, allowing each participant to light a candle in memory of someone. Close adult supervision is required to prevent sleeves from getting too close to the candles.

When each person has had a turn, say, "We light these candles to honor those we have loved. May they live in our memories forever. So be it."

Extinguish the candles. The children can take home the candles and the pictures they brought with them. They may also take home any pictures, stories, or clay objects they made during Choices Time.

Evaluation and Planning

Did the children appear comfortable in discussion and during the candle lighting? If any anxieties appear to have been aroused in any of the children, talk with their parents about it as soon as possible.

Did parents talk with you about resources and/or the children's expriences with death?

Decide which session will follow next. Are there ways this session could be related to the next one?

If your next class is Session 10, Thanksgiving Day, be sure to read the entire session and mail a letter (see Resource 11) to each participant before the session meets.

We Each Have Our Precious Memories

Words: Patricia Hoertdoerfer
Music: "We Are Dancing Sarah's Circle"

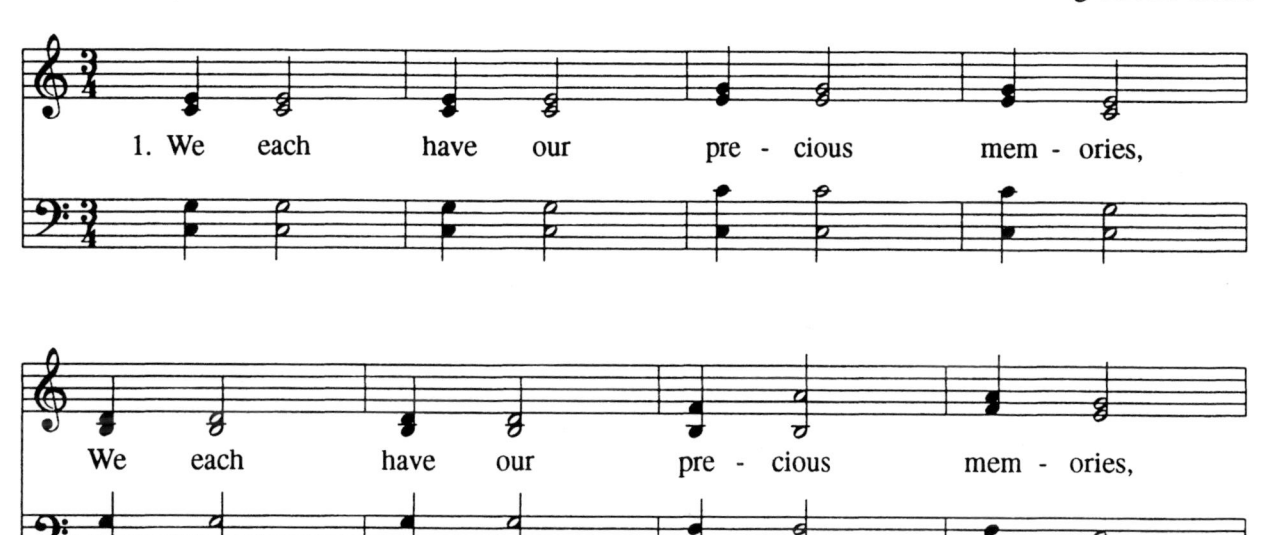

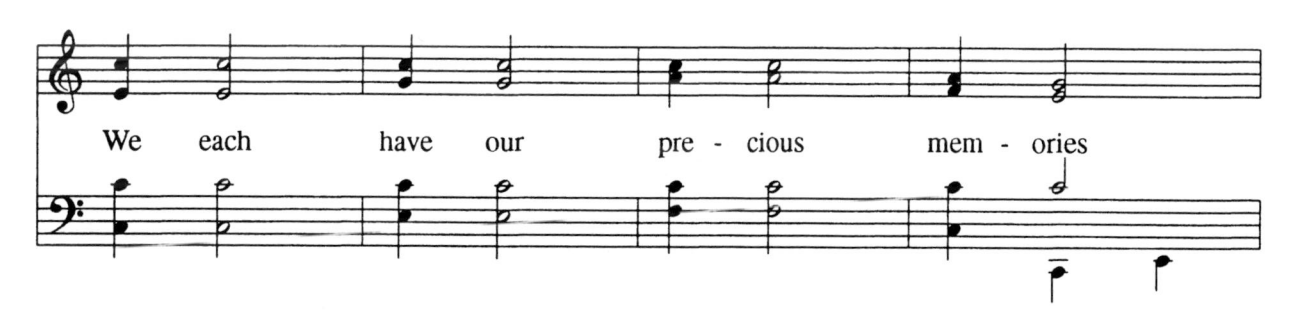

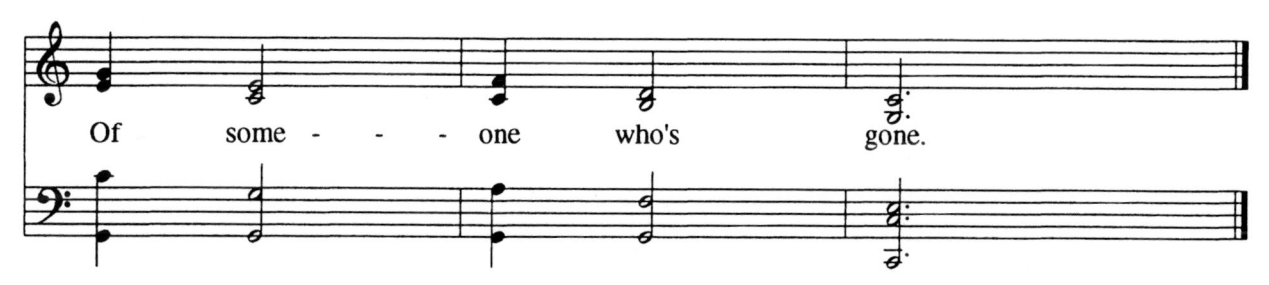

1. We each have our precious memories,
   We each have our precious memories,
   We each have our precious memories
   Of someone who's gone.

2. Birth to death to birth, the circle,
   Birth to death to birth, the circle,
   Birth to death to birth, the circle
   In this life we share.

3. On and on the circle's moving,
   On and on the circle's moving,
   On and on the circle's moving
   In this life we share.

Session 9: A Time to Remember Those Who Have Died

10 A Time to Give Thanks— Thanksgiving Day

Goals for Participants

- To become aware of many things to be thankful for.
- To learn that thanksgiving celebrations happen in many places in the world.

Materials

- Copies of Resource 11, "Thanksgiving Letter to Families of the *Special Times* Class," for each participant
- Pictures of thanksgiving feasts and celebrations from picture and storybooks.
- Snapshot of class in sukkah (if available) from Session 5.
- Stickers of cornucopia of food and other seasonal symbols and scenes
- Half-sheets of heavy paper
- Markers
- Colored gift-wrap paper (white on underside)
- Transparent tape
- Popcorn (or ingredients and equipment to make it)
- Camera and film to photograph the children at the celebration
- Celebration candles
- Chalice, candle, and matches
- Books about Thanksgiving and Sukkot for the Reading Corner, such as:
  Earth Festivals, by Delores LaChapelle and Janet Bourque
  An Old-Fashioned Thanksgiving, by Louisa May Alcott
  The First Thanksgiving Feast, by Joan Anderson
  Earth Prayers from Around the World, edited by Elizabeth Roberts and Elias Amidon
  Thanksgiving Day, by Gail Gibbons
  The Thanksgiving Book, written and illustrated by Frank Jupo

Preparation

- Read through the entire session plan and decide who will lead each part of the session.

- Early in the week, make copies of Resource 11 for each participant and mail them before the session meets.

- Make a sign, "*Special Times* celebrates today Thanksgiving," for the Unitarian Universalist poster.

- Prepare to tell or read the story, "The Gift of Joy."

- Prepare or arrange with a music attendant to teach the Thanksgiving song, "Give Thanks Together," to be sung during the Song activity and with parents during the Closing.

- Copy the words to the song and the closing words onto newsprint.

- If you are making popcorn during this session, plan your schedule accordingly.

- Cut gift-wrap paper (white on underside) into 6" squares, one for each person who will attend the celebration.

- Make the necessary arrangements for the Thanksgiving celebration with families: table decorations, paper goods, celebration candles, etc.

- Prepare and obtain all necessary materials for activities and Special Corners.

Background

Many stories are told of the origins of Thanksgiving Day. In Canada, Martin Frobisher landed his ship safely in Newfoundland in 1568 and conducted a religious ceremony in thanksgiving for the event. This is usually considered the first Canadian Thanksgiving.

In 1879, an official day of Thanksgiving was proclaimed by the government of Canada for the country: 'a day of Thanksgiving to Almighty God for the bountiful harvest with which Canada has been blest.' In England, Thanksgiving celebrations were called Harvest Home and in Scotland they were called Kern.

In Virginia, it is said that British colonists there celebrated earlier than 1621, which was the time of the Pilgrims' first Thanksgiving feast in Massachusetts. They celebrated the first harvest with turkey, squash, cranberries, and an Indian pudding made of corn meal and molasses boiled in a bag. The Pilgrims' celebration may have been inspired by Hebrew Bible stories of the Feast of Booths (Sukkot).

Although originally a harvest festival of the kind common to agricultural societies, Thanksgiving is celebrated today in the United States and Canada as a day of general thanksgiving for all of life's blessings. In Canada, Thanksgiving is observed around the 12th of October, and in the United States on the fourth Thursday in November.

Native Americans celebrated Thanksgiving as a natural part of their way of life. They gave thanks to the plants and animals as well as the sun and rain for providing them with food to nourish their bodies. Their feasts of thanksgiving varied according to the time and place. The Inuit story in this session celebrates the joy of the festival.

Session Plan

Gathering   Varies

As the children arrive, chat with them about how their families celebrate Thanksgiving. Give them Thanksgiving stickers and invite them to decorate the *Special Times* sign for the poster. Hang the poster on the classroom door.

Focusing   10 minutes

Gather in a circle in chairs or on a rug. If you have already done the session on Sukkot, show any pictures you have of the children in the sukkah. Invite the children to talk about what they remember of that day.

Then show pictures depicting Thanksgiving celebrations from books you have collected, usually the pictures are of people feasting. When showing a picture of the Pilgrims' first Thanksgiving, you might mention, "Some people think the Pilgrims were actually thinking about the Jewish feast of Sukkot when they celebrated their first Thanksgiving."

Conversation and Story   20 minutes

Introduce the story by saying something like, "Long, long ago, before the people from across the oceans came to North America, people have held feasts and festivals to show their thanks for food they have grown and gathered. The Native Americans who lived here held such celebrations long before the Pilgrims and other settlers came from England, Scotland, and Spain.

"Our story this morning is called 'The Gift of Joy,' and was told by Heather McDonald, a Canadian Unitarian Universalist religious educator. Her story is from the Inuit people who live at the edge of the northern forest in Canada."

Read the story, "The Gift of Joy."

Engage the children in a conversation about the things that make them happy—the magic of giving and receiving and the ways they show they are happy and thankful.

Talk about the celebration time they will have

later in this session with parents and family members. Would they like to give family members "notes of thanks" at the party? Do they want to sing the Thanksgiving song, "Give Thanks Together"? Should they end with a feast of popcorn? Keep them focused on making it their celebration for their families.

Song   5 minutes

Practice the Thanksgiving song, "Give Thanks Together," reminding them that they will sing it again with their families at the end of the session.

Activity   15 minutes

Engage the children in making individual notes of thanks and a cornucopia. Before the children start, talk about the things you are thankful for this Thanksgiving. Then ask them to talk about the things *they* are thankful for.

Give each child markers and a half-sheet of heavy paper. Invite them to write or draw something they are really thankful for, and tell them they can give these to their family members during the celebration time.

To make a cornucopia, bring two edges of the gift-wrap paper squares together (white paper inside) to form a cone. Overlap the edges and securely tape them together. Some children may want to work on these while others fill them with popcorn in the next activity.

Choices Time   Varies

As the children finish their projects, invite them to decorate the celebration table, pop the popcorn, and set a display of their notes of thanks.

Closing Circle   10 minutes

As the parents arrive, invite the children to give them their notes of thanks. Sing the Thanksgiving song together and eat the popcorn.

Take a group picture of the children to post with their Sukkot picture, or to use when Sukkot is celebrated. You may want other pictures of them with their families.

Light the candle and say something like, "We are thankful this day for many things—food and families, friends and pets, (include specific things the children drew in their notes) and for all good things. May we always be so."

Invite them to say the closing words together:

Were thanks with every gift expressed,
Each day would be Thanksgiving;
Were gratitude its very best,
Each life would be thanks living.
—Heather McDonald

Evaluation and Planning

What worked well? What could have been done better?

Plan for next week's session and decide which session will be used each week between now and Christmas time.

The Gift of Joy

An Inuit story as told by Heather McDonald

The story happens back at the beginning of things, but not at the *very* beginning. People already knew how to feed themselves by hunting animals of the land and sea, and how to make themselves clothes and houses and kayaks and whatever they needed. So they were comfortable enough, but never happy or excited. Every day was like every other day. People just went along doing what had to be done, and when they had finished their work they were so bored they went to sleep.

In that time there was a family who had three sons. The oldest son was old enough to go out hunting by himself—but one day he did not come back. And when the second son went hunting by himself, he too went out one day and never came home. So when Ermine, the third son, was old enough to go hunting, the parents worried about him. Ermine and his father were often separated as soon as they were away from the house, because Ermine always wanted to hunt caribou and his father wanted to go out on the water in his kayak.

One day, when Ermine was hunting caribou by himself, he saw a huge eagle flying high above him. The eagle began moving down, and although Ermine had an arrow ready, he did not shoot. The eagle landed near him and stood up as a man dressed in a cloak of eagle feathers.

"I have a gift for you," the Eagle Man said to Ermine. "It is a gift of joy, of festivals, of singing and dancing. I offered it to your two brothers. They did not take it, and therefore they never came home. If you wish to see your home again, you must take my gift, and promise to use it."

"I will take your gift," said Ermine, "but I don't really understand what it is. What is joy? What are festivals? What is singing? What is dancing?"

"Come to my house and find out," answered Eagle Man. So they turned their backs to the sea, and walked and walked toward the mountains. When they reached the mountains, they climbed and climbed and climbed. When they were nearly at the top of the highest mountain, Ermine could hear and feel a steady thud-thud-thud around them. "That is the beating of my mother's heart," said Eagle Man.

At the top of the mountain was the eagle's home. Eagle Man took Ermine inside, and Ermine saw Eagle Mother. She seemed very old and weak, but she looked bright and interested when Eagle Man said, "I have brought one of the people to learn from you about festivals and singing and dancing, and to receive the gift of joy. He will take this knowledge and this gift back to his own family, and in time to all the people.

So Eagle Mother began to teach Ermine. She taught him how to carefully build and decorate a special house for a festival. She showed him how to prepare delicious food, using ingredients and seasonings that were too rare to use often. Eagle Mother taught him how to make up songs about the world around him, about things that had happened to him, and things he had done. She sang so Ermine could learn how to add music, so that the words could be sung. Ermine also learned how to make a drum and beat out a rhythm that went with the song's music. He learned how to dance to the beat of the drum.

While Ermine was learning all these new things, something wonderful was growing inside him. It was the new feeling of joy—a feeling that made him so happy he could hardly wait to share it with all his family.

At last Eagle Mother said, "You are ready. Go home, get ready for your festival, and invite many guests to share it with you."

"But we don't know any other people," said Ermine.

"Human people are lonely and do not know each other because they have not yet received the gift of joy," said Eagle Mother. "Do not be afraid. Prepare your festival. You will find when the time comes that there are many guests to invite. But there is one more thing before you go. I have given you much, and it is proper that you should give me a present in return. What would really please me would be some sinew string."

At first Ermine was worried. There were no caribou to hunt up on top of this mountain, so where would he get sinew string? Then he remembered that all his arrow points were tied to the arrows with sinew string, so he quickly untied them and gave the strings to Eagle Mother. Eagle Man changed himself to a huge eagle again, and told Ermine to climb onto his back and hold tight. They flew back to the place where they had first met, and after saying good-bye to Eagle Man, Ermine went back to his house.

There Ermine told his father and mother all that had happened to him. He explained how he had been given the gifts of celebration and joy to share with all people. Then Ermine told his parents that he would start getting ready for the first festival at once. When the time came, there would be many guests to invite.

His parents could make no sense of what he was talking about, but they did understand that if he had not made a promise to the eagles he would have never come home again. They knew that Ermine must keep his word.

So they set to work at once to help Ermine get ready for the first festival. As they helped him and he taught them, they began to have a new feeling—they were *enjoying* what they were doing. They were lively and happy as they set up their feast hall, made up songs and dances, tried new tastes and ways of preparing things to eat. They no longer fell asleep because they were bored. Instead, there didn't seem to be enough hours in the day for all they wanted to do. And they talked about how next time it would be even better, because they would search out some other families and teach them about festivals. This might be difficult, because people lived rather far apart in those days, but now it seemed well worth the effort.

All along, of course, they had been looking forward to the day when everything was ready for inviting the guests—even though they couldn't imagine where these would come from. But sure enough, when Ermine went outside on that special day, there were people all around, richly dressed in beautiful furs, and he invited them at once into the feast hall.

There they stayed the rest of that day, and all through the night. They ate and said everything was delicious. They joined in songs and dances. They talked together and gave each other presents. At times things got so noisy that the eagles might have heard it on their mountain top, but it was a joyful noise.

At dawn the guests thanked Ermine and his mother and father, and began to walk toward the forest. As they went among the trees, they suddenly changed backed into wolves, lynxes, foxes, bears, and all the other forest animals. The eagles had sent them to be their first guests, and the power of joy was strong enough to change them into human beings for that festival time.

A while later, Ermine met his friend Eagle Man again, and they went to the eagle's mountain home because Eagle Mother wanted to see Ermine again. When she came out to greet them, Ermine was surprised to see that she was young and strong. Eagle Mother explained that when humans celebrate joyfully, old eagles grow young again.

The people always remembered that the eagles had given them the gift of joy, and honoured the eagles at their time of song, dance, and merrymaking.

Give Thanks Together

Words & Music: Traditional

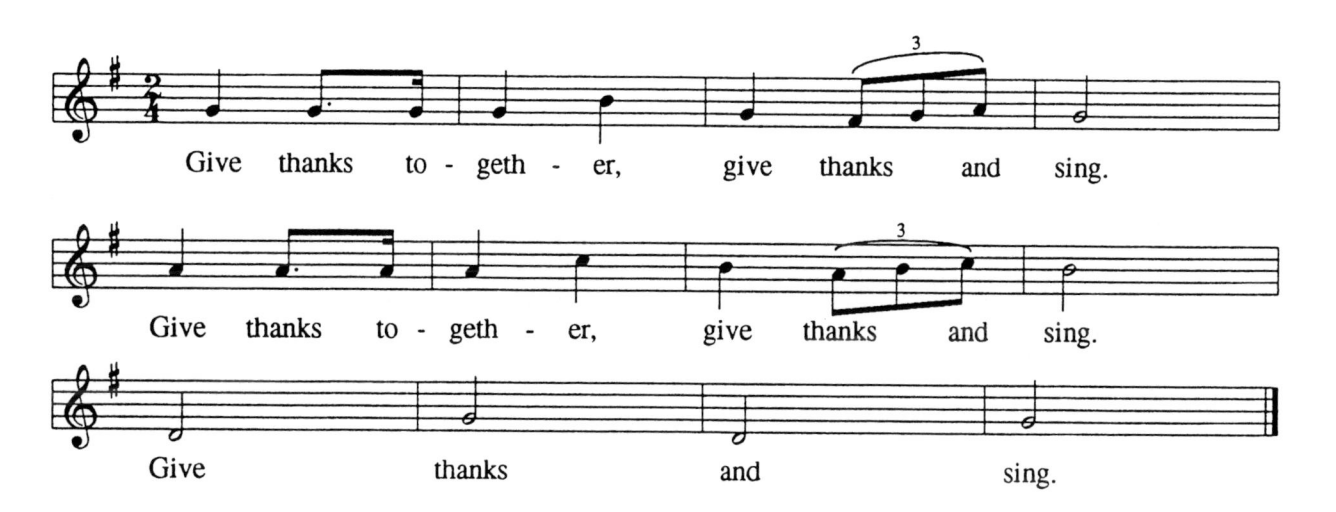

Give thanks to - geth - er, give thanks and sing.

Give thanks to - geth - er, give thanks and sing.

Give thanks and sing.

11 A Time for Freedom of Worship—Hanukkah

Goals for Participants

- To learn about the origins of Hanukkah.
- To learn how the lighting of lamps and candles is common to various winter holidays.
- To enjoy celebrating the Jewish Festivals of Lights.

Materials

- Stickers of Hanukkah menorah, Jewish star, and candle
- Tape of Hanukkah music
- Cassette player
- Hanukkah (8-branched) menorah and Hanukkah candles
- Matches
- Pictures of distinctive menorahs
- Posterboard
- Scissors and transparent tape
- Markers
- Peanuts, raisins, or Hanukkah gelt (chocolate money)
- Latkes and applesauce (or ingredients to make latkes if time permits; you will need potatoes, eggs, flour, oil, salt, and pepper) or jelly doughnuts
- Jewish holiday books and illustrated Jewish calendars for the Reading Corner. Include the following books:
  Hanukka, Eight Nights, Eight Lights, by Malka Drucker
  A Picture Book of Jewish Holidays, by David Adler
  Hanukkah: The Festival of Lights, by Jenny Korelak

Preparation

- Read through the entire session and decide who will lead each part.
- Make a sign, "*Special Times* celebrates today Hanukkah" for the Unitarian Universalist poster.
- Prepare to read or tell the story, "A Great Miracle," for the Conversation and Story activity.
- Decide if you will re-enact "A Great Miracle" and gather the appropriate materials for children to make shields and simple props.
- Plan your snack of jelly doughnuts or latkes (potato pancakes) and applesauce. Latkes can be made ahead of time and re-heated. If there is time to make them in the classroom, you will need an electric skillet or griddle and pancake turner. The recipe is included in Choices Time.
- Trace the dreidel pattern from Resource 12 onto cardboard; prepare one for each child.
- Obtain all materials and resources for activities and Special Corners.

Background

The joyful Hanukkah celebration of the Jewish people occurs in December, usually at the same time as the Christmas season. Traditionally, it commemorates the rededication of the Temple at Jerusalem. Hanukkah was first celebrated over 2,000 years ago after the Jews, under the leadership of Judah the Maccabee (the Hammer), recaptured the Temple from the Syrians. Because the Syrians had occupied and defiled the Temple, it had to be ritually cleansed. Also, the Jews needed to find oil for the sacred lamp. According to legend, the Jews found only one jug of oil which was enough for the lamp to burn just one night. But it burned in the lamp for eight days and nights. These eight days and nights became the Hanukkah festival, which Jewish people have celebrated ever since in many lands and under many different circumstances.

The story also says that when the victorious Jews first entered the Temple, they found eight iron spurs abandoned by the Syrians in their flight. On these spurs the Jews stuck eight candles and the light was the origin of the special menorah (candlestick) which burns during the festival.

Hanukkah has usually been celebrated more in the home than in the synagogue. On each night of Hanukkah, the family gathers around the menorah and lights and blesses the festive candles—one on the first night, two the second, and so on, until in the final evening all eight are burning. They exchange gifts, play dreidel games, eat latkes, and retell the story of the victory of the Maccabees and the little jug of oil that burned for eight days.

Session Plan

Gathering   Varies

Play Hanukkah music and as the children arrive, greet them and ask them to decorate the Jewish Calendar and the *Special Times* sign with Hanukkah stickers. Hang the poster on the classroom door. Then invite them to look at the menorahs as you point out the number of branches/candles.

Focusing   10 minutes

With everyone seated in a circle, light the candles in the Hanukkah menorah. Say, "How many candles are on the menorah?" Explain that of the nine candles, the one in the middle is called the *shammash* or servant. Then say, "This is a Hanukkah menorah. It is different from other menorahs, which have only seven candles.

Conversation and Story   15 minutes

Say something like, "Does anyone know the story of why the Hanukkah menorah has eight candles plus the servant candle? Can you guess why the one in the middle is the *shammash*?" Allow time for responses. Perhaps someone will know that the *shammash* is used to light the others.

Then say, "Let's hear the story that tells us about the miracle of Hanukkah."

Read the story, "A Great Miracle."

Activity   20 minutes

This can overlap with Choices Time.

A most popular Hanukkah game is dreidel. The dreidel is a spinning top and means "turn." On the sides of the dreidel are the four Hebrew letters:

נ ג ה ש

Nun   Gimmel   Hey   Shin

They stand for the words, *Nes Gadol Hayah Sham*, which means "A great miracle happened there."

Tell the children that they will be making dreidels and playing a game.

To make the dreidels, have the children go to the craft table and find their cardboard patterns. Assist the children in cutting out their dreidels, folding and taping or gluing them together, and fitting the small turners into the tops to enable them to spin.

When all the children have assembled their dreidels, invite them to a play area. Pass out an equal number of nuts, raisins, or Hanukkah gelt to each child. Then play the dreidel game with the following rules.

Each player puts one peanut, raisin, or gelt piece in the center. Then the first player spins the dreidel. If it lands on:

Nun—the player does nothing
Gimmel—the player takes everything in the center

Session 11: A Time for Freedom of Worship

Hey—the player takes half
Shin—the player puts one item in

Before the next player spins, everyone puts another piece in the center.

Choices Time   Varies

As the children finish their dreidels, point out the choices available: Reading Corner, Craft Center to make simple props—shields, torah, menorah, etc.—to aid retelling of the Hanukkah story, and the food preparation area if you are cooking latkes.

Recipe for Latkes
3 grated potatoes
1 grated onion (optional—but you may need to adjust other ingredients if not used)
2 beaten eggs
2 tablespoons flour
1 teaspoon salt
vegetable oil for frying

Mix all ingredients together. Drop by spoonfuls onto hot, oiled surface of skillet or griddle. Brown on both sides. Serve with applesauce.

Closing Circle   5 minutes

After eating the latkes and applesauce or jelly doughnuts, gather in a circle. If you choose, re-enact the Hanukkah story with players, simple props, and a storyteller. Then re-light the first Hanukkah candle. (If this is the third day of Hanukkah, for example, light the first three. Remember to place them from the right, light from the left.)

Say something like, "We light these candles for freedom to worship. We are thankful for this precious right, and for our Unitarian Universalist congregation where we may worship together. Shalom."

Extinguish the candles.

Evaluation and Planning

What went well today?

What session will be used next? Did this session fall between Advent and Christmas? If so, how can continuity be resumed?

A Great Miracle

A long time ago, more than 2,000 years ago, the Jews had been defeated by a people called the Syrians.

When Antiochus IV became king of Syria, he was angry at the Jewish people for refusing to worship the Greek gods that he worshiped.

The Jews believed they should worship their own god, in their own way. (Ask the children, "What do you think?" Allow time for responses.)

Most of us don't want anyone to tell us what to think, or what to say, or what we should consider important. We believe that we have the right to worship in our own way, and that others should have the same right.

But Antiochus didn't believe that, and he decided to make the Jews worship his gods. He forbade them to read their holy books, pray to their god, and celebrate their holidays.

Antiochus even had Greek statues put in the Temple in Jerusalem, the holiest of all places to the Jews! He ordered the Jews to give up their Sabbath.

The Jews did not like this at all.

In the village of Modin, a leader rose up and his name was Mattathias. He and his five sons—Judah Maccabee, Jonathan, Johanah, Eleazar, and Simon—joined a band of patriots in the hills, and became guerilla fighters. On dark nights, they laid low the armies of Antiochus, one after another. When Mattathias died, Judah become the leader of the outlaw army, and it was under his leadership that they entered Jerusalem. When they reached the Holy City, their joy turned to bitterness when they saw the dirt and the desolation in the temple area. They started to work on restoring and scrubbing the Temple, and on the 25th of Kislev, they re-lit the Great Menorah with the small bit of holy oil they had found. Every year thereafter, the Jews celebrate this day as the Festival of Cleansing of the Temple.

From here, the story goes into a number of legends. The most loved story is one in which there is only enough oil for one day, but by a miracle, it burned for eight days, until more oil could be found and sanctified.

So for eight days, they celebrated the dedication of the Temple and their right to worship freely. And ever since that time, Jews everywhere have celebrated that great event that happened long ago. On the eight days of Hanukkah—which actually means "dedication"—Jewish people light candles, sing songs, play games, eat foods fried in oil, and give one another gifts! Even when Jews have lived in places where again it was against the law for them to worship freely, they have celebrated in this way.

(At this point, bring out the menorah and place the candles in it, one at a time, beginning at the right. Then, lighting the candles from the left, tell the children that one candle is lit the first evening of Hanukkah, two the second evening, and so on up to eight candles for each day of Hanukkah.)

Hanukkah *is* a celebration that we Unitarian Universalists can all appreciate, because we believe that all people should be free to worship in their own way.

12 A Time for Getting Ready—Advent

Goals for Participants

- To enrich their understanding of Christmas by focusing on the birth of Jesus.
- To appreciate that sometimes it is necessary to wait and prepare for good things to happen, such as the birth of a baby.
- To become aware of some of the elements of waiting—expectation and hope—as well as some of the elements of preparation—service and cooperation.

Materials

- Copies of Resource 13, "Advent Calendar Pattern," Resource 15, "Advent List of Activities," and Resource 16, "Advent Letter to Parents," for each participant
- Three copies of Resource 14, "Advent Pocket Decorations," reduced to half size, for each participant
- Tape of Christmas music
- Cassette player
- Advent wreath/candleholders with four candles
- Stickers of candles, empty Christmas stockings, undecorated trees, advent wreaths, barns, empty cradles
- 9 x 12" sheets of construction paper in green, red, and other colors
- Cardboard sheets at least 12 x 15"
- Pencils
- Scissors
- White glue
- Extra large envelopes
- Nativity set, suitable for children to play with; use only the stable and animals which might live in a barn. (Save Mary, Joseph, baby, shepherds, sheep, angels, camels, and kings for later sessions.)
- Shiny paper and glittery trimmings for Craft Center
- Books for the Reading Corner, such as:
  A Time to Keep: The Tasha Tudor Book of Holidays, written and illustrated by Tasha Tudor
  Who Is Coming to Our House?, by Joseph Slate
  Celebrations, by Myra Cohn Livingston
  Christmas In the Stable, by Astrid Lindgren
  Christmas In a Barn, by Margaret Wise Brown

Preparation

- Read through the entire session and decide who will lead each section.

- Make a sign, "*Special Times* celebrates *Advent* today," for the Unitarian Universalist poster.

- Buy or make an Advent wreath. To make one, use a wire ring and stuff with evergreen sprigs and holly. Use clip-on candleholders. The four candles may be all white, or three purple and one pink.

- To make the Advent calendar for each participant, enlarge Leader Resource 13 to a 12 x 12" wreath and photocopy. Paste the copies to cardboard, and cut out the wreaths. Set them aside for the children to complete.

- Cut green construction paper into 24 squares (1 1/2" each); number the squares from 1 to 24. Make 24 squares for each child.

- Prepare Resource 16, which is a letter to parents, for the children to take home with their Advent calendars.

- Purchase enough extra large envelopes for each child and write their names on the front.

- Obtain the nativity set and other necessary materials for activities and Special Corners.

Background

The word Advent, which means "coming," was originally used for the Coming of the Christ, and applied only to that day. After the sixth century, its meaning was expanded to include the whole period of preparation for this day—as it is now.

The Advent season marks the beginning of the Christian church year. The orthodox Christian church year is based on the three main incidents in the life of Jesus—Christmas, Easter, and Pentecost—which form the framework of the Christian year. Each of these great festivals was preceded by a period of preparation to enable Christians to meditate on the spiritual significance of these events in the life of Jesus.

Although the birth of Jesus, or the Nativity, is the major holy day, the four Sundays of Advent are recognized as the Advent season, a time of expectation and quiet reflection. Advent begins on the Sunday nearest November 30, St. Andrew's Day. For Unitarian Universalists, Advent means less than it does for more traditional Christians. However, Advent can provide an opportunity to deepen our awareness of the spiritual values inherent in the winter festival season.

The use of the Advent wreath originated a few hundred years ago among Lutherans in Germany. The wreaths are made of evergreens and are either suspended from the ceiling or placed on a table. Four candles are fastened in holders to the wreath, representing the four weeks of Advent.

On the first Sunday of Advent one candle is lit and allowed to burn during a ceremony of readings, prayers, and songs. On each of the following Sundays an additional candle is lit at the beginning of the ceremony until the fourth Sunday when all four are lit. Candle colors have varied over the years: some churches use white liturgical candles, others use three purple candles signifying repentance and one pink signifying joy (third Sunday). Sometimes on Christmas Eve a large candle is lit in the center of the wreath to symbolize Christ, the light of the world.

For children in our culture, the weeks approaching Christmas are often fraught with stress, as the media, the retail sector, and even the schools build up an ever-increasing sense of anticipation and excitement. Some families observe both Hannukah and Christmas, which can create even more excitement. We can help children deal more constructively with these pressures by focusing on an attitude of quiet preparation and patience. Also, these activities help them to see that they can play an active and cooperative role in getting ready for Christmas.

Session Plan

Gathering   Varies

As the children arrive, have Christmas music playing softly. Greet them individually and hand them some Christmas stickers to decorate the Christian Calendar and the *Special Times* sign on the poster. Hang the poster on the classroom door. You might start a conversation, asking why the tree is undecorated or why the stocking or the cradle is empty.

Focusing   5 minutes

Gather everyone into a circle. Show the Advent wreath with its four candles, then light the first candle. Say something like, "This is our Advent wreath, and we light the first candle in anticipation of the special times of this Christmas season."

Conversation   15 minutes

Say, "As we get ready for the holidays, we all get very excited, don't we? We anticipate—look forward to—something really wonderful happening. That excitement and anticipation are the reasons we light our first Advent candle."

Ask the children what they anticipate in the holidays, and allow time for responses.

Then say, "Have you ever waited a long, long time for something to happen? Like your birthday, or the first day of school in the fall, or the last day of school in the spring, or company to come, or Christmas, or for a new baby?

"Your parents know what it's like to wait for a baby to be born! There are lots of things you have to do to get ready for a baby. You can't just wait until it comes to think about what will be needed: a place to sleep, diapers, some little shirts and other clothes, maybe bottles, a backpack or a stroller. Certainly you have to have a blanket and a bed for the baby at home! You need all these things, whether the baby is being born into the family or adopted.

"And if the baby is being born into the family, the mother does things to take care of herself and the baby while it is growing. Often the mother and father go to special classes to learn the best way of bringing the baby into the world.

"Sometimes it seems as if waiting for a new baby takes a long time and a lot of work. But the special, wonderful joy of having that new baby in the family makes all that waiting, and planning, and getting ready worthwhile!

"We have lots of things to do to get ready for Christmas, too, don't we? What are some of these things?" Allow time for responses. The children may mention some of these things: making or buying Christmas cards, making or buying gifts, and wrapping gifts, putting up a Christmas tree, baking cookies, cleaning, and decorating the house.

Continue, "And if your family celebrates Hanukkah, too, that's even more preparation. People your age can do lots of things to help the family get ready for the holidays. What are some of the things you could do?" Allow time for responses.

Then say, "These four weeks when we look forward to Christmas are called Advent. It is a time when we do things to get ready for Christmas. We get ready in our homes and churches, and we get ready in our hearts and minds. Advent is a time to celebrate the wonder of birth, the power of love, and the sacredness of all life."

Activity — 25 minutes

Say to the children, "While you are waiting for Christmas, you might like to have a special Advent calendar to help you see how quickly the days go by as you help get ready for the holidays. The one we will make today looks like an Advent wreath with a decoration on it for each day leading up to Christmas."

Have each child take 24 pocket squares that you made out of green construction paper and an Advent calendar pattern. Show them how to glue three sides of each square and attach them to the wreath to make a pocket that opens at the top. Make sure they match each numbered pocket to the corresponding number on the wreath.

Hand out copies of Resource 14 so the children can cut out some Advent decorations and glue them to the outside of the pocket, but be sure that the number is still showing.

Then help them carefully cut apart the list of activities on Resource 15 so that each activity is on a separate strip of paper. Fold each strip and tuck into the appropriate pockets.

Play Christmas music on the cassette player while the children are working on their Advent calendars, or sing Christmas carols that are traditionally sung in your congregation during this season.

Put each child's Advent calendar in an extra large envelope for them to take home. Include a copy of Resource 16. Explain that they are to open the pockets and do an activity each day.

Choices Time — Varies

Point out the choices: books, materials for making holiday cards, and the nativity set. Some children may continue to work on their Advent calendars.

Closing Circle — 5 minutes

Gather around the Advent Wreath. Re-light the first candle for "anticipation." Unless it will interfere with your schedule for other Sundays, you may wish to light the second candle for "preparation." Say something like, "As we go from our group today, we are excited and filled with anticipation for the holidays to come. Let's remember to use our energy and excitement to help with the preparations for the holidays. Go in hope, joy, and peace."

Evaluation and Planning

Will Christmas Eve be the next session, or will others intervene? Often Hanukkah will be used between the two.

Plan to make connections with the Advent/Hanukkah/Christmas sessions—according to the order you use.

13 A Time for Joy to be Born—Christmas Eve

Goals for Participants

- To know the traditional Christmas story of the birth of Jesus as a source of joy and wonder.
- To gain a Unitarian Universalist understanding of Christmas that "each night a child is born is a holy night."

Materials

- Copies of Resource 18, "Each Night a Child is Born is a Holy Night" by Sophia Lyon Fahs, for each participant
- Stickers of angels, stars, shepherds, mother, and child
- Tape of Christmas music
- Cassette player
- Nativity set: stable, Mary, Joseph, the baby Jesus, barn animals, shepherds, sheep, and angels (save The Three Kings and camels for the session on Epiphany)
- Words and music to familiar Christmas carols, such as "Silent Night," "O Little Town of Bethlehem," "O Come All Ye Faithful," "Hark The Herald Angels Sing," "Joy To The World," "It Came Upon The Midnight Clear," "The Friendly Beasts," including carols that your congregation will sing during worship services throughout this season
- Used Christmas cards with nativity scenes, angels, and shepherds
- Posterboard, cardboard, and colored paper
- Scissors
- White glue
- Markers, pens, and pencils
- Craft Center: additional materials (stamps and ink pads, fabrics, yarn, glitter, etc.) for making Christmas cards
- Chalice, candle, and matches
- Books that re-tell the Christmas story, for the Reading Corner, such as:
  A New Day, by Don Bolognese
  Christmas in the Barn, by Margaret Wise Brown
  Christmas in the Stable, by Astrid Lindgren
  The Christmas Pageant: From the Text of Matthew and Luke, retold and illustrated by Tomie de Paola
  A Child Is Born: The Christmas Story, by Elizabeth Winthrop
  Celebrations, by Myra Cohn Livingston and Leonard Everett Fisher (A good poem to read from this book is "Christmas Eve.")

Preparation

- Read through the entire session and decide who will lead each part.

- Make a sign, "*Special Times* celebrates today *Christmas Eve,*" for the Unitarian Universalist poster.

- Prepare to tell or read "The Story of the Birth of Jesus" for the Conversation and Story activity.

- Learn any unfamiliar songs you plan to sing.

- Obtain or prepare all needed materials for activities and Special Corners.

Background

The essence of the Christmas story is the birth of the baby Jesus. No one knows at what time of the year Jesus was born. Long after his death, stories of Jesus' birth were collected and written down. The growing Christian Church wanted to celebrate his birth, and the church fathers decided that it should be during the most beloved and universal festivals celebrated by people around the world. The time of mid-winter celebrations—festivals of light—was decreed as the time to celebrate the birth of Jesus Christ—Christmas.

Old festivals and customs were added to the new celebrations of the Christmas story, of the child born in a manger, of shepherds and wise men who visited the manger, and of angels and heavenly hosts who sang and proclaimed the birth. Stories were gathered from many places and times and woven into story and song and poetry that is the magic of Christmas.

Unitarian Universalists are often concerned about interpreting the Christmas festival and all the legends and symbols that have grown up around the story of the birth of Jesus. You may wish to read the story from the Bible. There are two versions in the Gospels: Matthew 1:18-2:12 and Luke 2:1-20.

Or you may wish to tell the Christmas story with natural simplicity emphasizing the wonders of birth and the power of love. *Christmas In the Stable* or *Christmas in the Barn* are excellent books with this interpretation for young children. Another possible way of telling the Christmas story is to place it next to the birth stories of Buddha and Confucius as they appear in *From Long Ago and Many Lands,* edited by Sophia Lyon Fahs.

In this session there is a simple version of the Christmas story. You can select another story or stories you feel is most appropriate to the families in your religious education program and Unitarian Universalist congregation. Remember that it is very difficult for a child of this age to distinguish between fact and symbolic meanings. The messages of hope in times of darkness, hope in a violent world for peace on earth and good will to all people, and the importance and promise of every child born into this world are the central meanings of the Christmas story.

Session Plan

Gathering   Varies

As the children arrive, have Christmas music playing and greet them individually. Hand out the Christmas stickers and invite the children to decorate the Christian Calendar and the *Special Times* sign for the poster. Hang the poster on the classroom door. Remind the children of the meaning of Advent by pointing out a sticker on the *Special Times* sign from the Advent session. Ask them how they are helping and preparing for the holidays.

Focusing   5 minutes

Gather everyone in a circle around the nativity scene, set up with only the stable, barn animals, and empty cradle. Say something like, "You remember that during Advent, we have been waiting and getting ready for Christmas. The time of getting ready comes to an end on Christmas Eve. That's the special time we are celebrating today." Invite the children to place Mary, Joseph, and the baby in the scene.

Conversation and Story   15 minutes

Ask, "What happens on Christmas Eve?" Allow time for responses. The children may say that Jesus was born on Christmas Day. This would be a good time to point out that Christian holidays, like Jewish ones, originally began on the evening, or "eve," before the day.

Then say, "Of course, no one knows for sure when Jesus was really born, or where, but we celebrate the Christmas story, and there is always more to a story than just the facts."

Read "The Story of the Birth of Jesus."

When the story is finished, invite comments and then ask the children to place the shepherds and sheep and angels in the nativity scene. Then suggest singing some songs to celebrate this joyous and wonderful birth.

Song   5-10 minutes

Sing carols you have chosen.

Activity   10 minutes

Invite the children to make their own Christmas collages by cutting out pictures from old Christmas cards and gluing them onto cardboard or posterboard. They may also wish to use markers to add words or drawings of their own.

Choices Time   10 minutes

Point out the choices available: the nativity set, books, and card-making materials. Some children may wish to dramatize the story.

Closing Circle   5 minutes

Gather the children in a circle and light the chalice candle. Read "Each Night a Child is Born is a Holy Night." This poem is often used in Christmas Eve services and/or dedications of infants, so you may be able to tell the children something about its use in your congregation.

Then say something like, "May the joy and wonder of the birth of the Christmas child be with us now and evermore. So be it. Amen."

Evaluation and Planning

What worked well?

When will the next session be? If your program is in session the week following Christmas, you may choose to have one of the sessions designed for "Anytime" and save Epiphany until January.

The Story of the Birth of Jesus

by Aloyse Hume

Once, a long, long time ago—before you were born—another baby was born. The story is that the baby's mother, Mary, and his father, Joseph, had to leave their home city of Nazareth and go on business to the town of Bethlehem. To go from Nazareth to Bethlehem Joseph walked, but Mary, who was going to have a child soon, rode on a little donkey. They reached Bethlehem late in the evening and went to the inn to ask for a room for the night. But the town was crowded with people, and the innkeeper told them that there was no more room at the inn, and that they would have to find another place to stay. At last Mary and Joseph found shelter in a small barn with the animals. When the baby was born that night, Mary said, "His name will be Jesus," and she wrapped him warmly and laid him in a manger. There he went to sleep.

That night there were shepherds in a field nearby looking after their sheep. And suddenly there was a bright light all about them, and an angel came to them. The shepherds were afraid, but the angel said, "Fear not, for I bring you good news for all people. On this day, there is born in Bethlehem a child, and you will find him warmly wrapped and lying in a manger." And then there were, not one angel, but many angels saying:

"Glory to God in the highest, and on earth peace, good will toward all people." And the shepherds went to Bethlehem and found Mary and Joseph and the baby lying in a manger.

There were also in that country three kings, who had seen a new star rise in the East and had followed it. The star seemed to come to rest just above the barn where the family was staying, and when the three kings entered there, they found Mary and Joseph and the baby Jesus. The kings remembered this very first birthday of Jesus by bringing him gifts. This story is a story of long, long ago, but this year, and every year, we still remember Jesus' birthday by giving gifts and by singing, like the angels:

"Glory to God in the highest, and on earth peace, good will toward all people."

14 A Time for Giving Gifts—Epiphany

Goals for Participants

- To learn the story of wise men bearing gifts.
- To experience the joy of making and giving a gift.
- To integrate their learning about *Special Times*.

Materials

- Stickers of camels, gifts, and crowns
- Nativity set: stable, Mary, Joseph, the baby Jesus, barn, animals, shepherds, sheep, angels, The Three Kings, and camels
- Inexpensive fabric for tablecloth
- Markers and fabric crayons
- Four calendars from Session 1 and/or the children's "About Me" posters
- Chalice, candles, and matches
- Books for the Reading Corner, such as: *The Story of the Three Wise Kings*, re-told and illustrated by Tomie de Paolo

Preparation

- Read through the entire session plan and decide who will lead each part.

- Make a sign "*Special Times* celebrates today *Epiphany*," for the Unitarian Universalist poster.

- Prepare to tell or read the story, "Visitors Appear, Carrying Gifts."

- This session plan includes decorating (with *Special Times* pictures) a cloth for the table used to hold the flaming chalice (or a flower table if your congregation does not use a chalice), either in the main worship room or the room used for children's worship. Discuss with your congregation's religious educator and/or minister where the gift will go and when and where it is to be presented. If the presentation is to be made at the end of this session, adjust the session plan accordingly.

- Prepare the cloth by cutting it to fit your designated table and either stitching a hem or gluing or stitching braid on the edges. Whether the table is round or rectangular, the cloth can be made with either a drop of about one foot, or it can fall to the floor. A runner which hangs off the ends of a rectangular table would also be appropriate. (If your group is large, you could also make a hanging for either the front of the pulpit or a wall of the worship room.) See Resource 18, "*Special Times* Chalice Tablecloth," for a diagram.

- If the presentation is to be made during this session, coordinate it with the religious education coordinator and the minister. Invite the minister(s), religious educators and chair, and board president to make presentations. Decide who will talk about the project and who will make the presentation.

- Obtain all other materials for activities and Special Corners.

Background

The Christian festival of Epiphany, celebrated on January 6, commemorates the appearance of the Magi/Three Wise Men/Three Kings bearing gifts for the newborn Jesus. Epiphany was first celebrated in the second century and is also known as Twelfth Night, Old Christmas, and Day of the Three Kings. It marks the end of the Christmas season.

"Epiphany" comes from the Greek word for "manifestation" or "appearance." The dictionary definitions of "epiphany" include a "revelatory manifestation of a divine being," and "a sudden intuitive perception of or insight into reality." Thus, the Feast of the Epiphany celebrates not only the appearance of The Three Kings but also, for Christians, the revelation of the divinity of Jesus to the Kings.

Epiphany marks and celebrates the coming of the Three Wise Men to the manger following the star of Bethlehem. It is said that it took them twelve days to reach Bethlehem. They were the kings or magi of the East who brought precious gifts to Jesus: Melchior, who came from Arabia, brought gold; Jaspar, from Tarsus, gave myrrh; and Balthasar, from Ethiopia, presented frankincense to the babe. Their gifts signified royalty, healing, and religion. Their coming from outside Palestine signified to Christians that Jesus' birth was good news for the whole world.

Session Plan

Gathering   Varies

Welcome the children back if there has been a break since your last session. Hand out stickers and invite the children to decorate the Christian Calendar and the *Special Times* sign for the poster. Hang the poster on the classroom door.

Focusing   5 minutes

Gather in a circle around the nativity set. Invite the children to add the camels and The Three Kings to the scene. Point out that the Kings are carrying gifts.

Conversation and Story   15 minutes

Talk about this time as a season for giving gifts. The children will probably respond by talking about gifts they *received* for Christmas. After allowing time for this kind of sharing, and perhaps mentioning a gift you received, shift the conversation to gift-giving by asking, "What did you give your brother/mother/father for Christmas?" Again, allow time for responses.

Then say, "It's fun to give gifts as well as to receive them. This morning, we will have an opportunity to make a gift for our congregation. But first, let's hear the story of The Three Kings, or The Three Wise Men, bearing gifts."

Read the story, "Visitors Appear, Carrying Gifts."

Activity   25 minutes

Say something like, "Today we will decorate a tablecloth for the table used to hold the chalice (describe). Later (or at the end of class) we will present it to our congregation as a gift from our class. Since we are celebrating special times, let's decorate it with pictures or symbols about some of the special times we are learning about."

Draw attention to the four calendars marked with special times you are celebrating and/or the "About Me" posters, on which the children drew or wrote about their favorite holidays. Encourage the children to illustrate many of the holidays, rather than all doing Christmas or birthdays.

Demonstrate how the cloth will fit on the table to show the children where the designs should go. The designs need to be placed near the bottom of the cloth. If the drop is short, be sure the designs do not run up onto the part that will be on the flat surface of the table. Some children may want to make a practice drawing on paper before they draw with markers or fabric crayons directly onto the cloth.

Choices Time   Varies

Point out the choices: Reading Corner and the nativity set. Some children may use this time to continue to work on the Chalice Tablecloth.

Closing Circle   5 minutes

Gather in a circle and light the chalice candle. Say something like, "Today we have talked about gifts received and gifts given. We have experienced the joy of making a gift for our congregation that will remind us (and others) of the special times we have celebrated—and are still celebrating during this year. As we move from these weeks of festivities into the winter months ahead, may we remember always to be cheerful givers and appreciative receivers of gifts. So be it."

Evaluation and Planning

What worked well? Could better planning have improved things? If the gift was not presented, plan for a time when that will be done.

What session will be next week?

Visitors Appear, Carrying Gifts

We've heard the story of how the baby Jesus was born in a stable, and how the shepherds heard the angels singing the news of his birth, and then went to the stable to see the child. People do like to visit new babies!

The story also says that a bright new star appeared in the sky, shining night after night over the stable where the baby Jesus was born. Far away, Three Wise Men—some people called them kings—saw this new star in the sky and decided to travel to where the star seemed to be shining.

Perhaps they expected to find kings, or at least wealthy people, when they arrived, for these Three Wise Men brought with them valuable gifts of gold, frankincense, and myrrh. Frankincense and myrrh were fragrant, wonderful smelling incense and oils. And everyone knows how valuable gold is.

For many years, people in that part of the world had been expecting a special king, a ruler sent by God to save the people. He was called a messiah. When they arrived at the stable on the Twelfth Night after the baby's birth, the Three Wise Men sensed there was something special about this child. They thought he might be the messiah, or at least a new king, and they gave this baby the royal gifts they had brought.

Of course, no one knows if any of this really happened, but it's a story that has lasted for almost 2,000 years.

When a new baby is born, anything seems possible.

Today, every year on the twelfth day after Christmas, we celebrate the coming of the Three Wise Men to visit the baby Jesus. We call this special day the Epiphany.

15 A Time to Plant Trees—Tu Bishvat

Goals for Participants

- To understand that trees are important to other forms of life on earth and to the earth itself.
- To understand that trees are also symbols of life.

Materials

- Baskets of fruit and nuts that might be grown in Israel
- Pictures of a variety of trees, including cypress and cedar trees, and others as shown in a guidebook
- Stickers of trees
- A copy of the video, audio-tape, or book, *The Man Who Planted Trees,* by Jean Giono
- TV and VCR or cassette player if video or audio-tape is used.
- Pencils
- Scissors
- White glue
- Planting materials, such as cups or pots, potting soil, water
- Seeds (avocado, dates, citrus)
- Chalice, candle, and matches
- Books about trees, Jewish holidays, and Israel for the Reading Corner

Preparation

- Read through the entire session plan; decide which activities you will use and who will lead them.

- Make a sign, "*Special Times* celebrates today Tu Bishvat," for the Unitarian Universalist poster.

- If you are interested in sending money to Israel for tree planting, or plan to plant your own tree outdoors, or want to take a tree walk, plan ahead and make all necessary arrangements. Adjust your schedule if necessary, and notify parents in advance if you would like their help driving to a park or want them to meet you there after the service.

- Obtain fruits and nuts. Choose from almonds, apples, apricots, avocados, bananas, bokser (fruit of the carob tree), citron (etrog), dates, figs, grapefruit, lemons, olives, papaya, peaches, pears, persimmons, pistachios, and pomegranates, or others which might grow in Israel.

- Practice the song, "Standing Like a Tree." Copy the lyrics on newsprint or the chalkboard to help the children learn the words.

- Review the activity options and decide which are feasible to do.
    If you plan a tree walk, recruit parents, other adults, or youth helpers to accompany you, with a ratio of one adult to four children. Map out the walk in advance
    If you will be planting a tree, make all arrangements well in advance, such as obtaining permission to plant a tree and deciding on a location; purchasing the tree and arranging for pick up or delivery; preparing soil and digging the hole; and recruiting adults to assist—probably from your Building and Grounds Committee.

- This session uses the book, *The Man Who Planted Trees,* by Jean Giono. Before the session, obtain a copy of the book, video, or audio-tape and familiarize yourself with the story.

Background

Tu Bishvat is the "New Year of the Trees." The name of the holiday is the Hebrew date, the 15th of Shevat (in January or February). The day signals the beginning of spring, and so trees are planted on this day in Israel. As the almond trees begin to blossom, people plant trees all around the country.

The Jewish people place both practical and symbolic importance on trees. Hebrew scripture prohibits the cutting of fruit trees, even during wartime (Deuteronomy 20), and in the Jewish tradition, the Torah is referred to as a "tree of life."

Long ago Jewish parents planted trees when a child was born—cedar for boys, cypress for girls. The cedar represented strength and height, the cypress tenderness and fragrance. When children grew up and were married, branches from each of their trees were cut and used for the canopy under which the couple stood during a wedding ceremony.

When the Jews were forced to leave Palestine, they continued to celebrate Tu Bishvat wherever they were, especially with fruits which reminded them of their ancient home land. Tu Bishvat has been a holiday of great importance to modern Israel, which has turned the desert into green and productive land with many trees and plants that are not native to the region. The importance of the day—and of trees themselves in Israeli culture—was underscored during the 1991 Persian Gulf war, when the Israeli prime minister planted a tree on Tu Bishvat at a time when Israel was under attack.

If you would like to purchase trees to be planted in Israel and you live in the US or Canada, send contributions to: The Jewish National Fund, 42 East 69th Street, New York, NY 10020. Call 1-800-542-TREE for current costs. (Credit cards accepted only with purchase of five or more trees.)

If you live in the US and want membership in the Arbor Day Foundation, send $15 to: National Arbor Day Foundation, 100 Arbor Avenue, Nebraska City, NE 68410. They will send you 10 small trees for planting, or the trees may be contributed to ongoing education projects.

In this session the central experience is the planting of trees. Reading *The Man Who Planted Trees* reminds us of our connection to the land and nature and the difference one person can make. Introducing children to the tradition of giving money to plant trees in Israel, or becoming involved in a local tree planting, helps them to see and to celebrate trees as symbols of life. It is customary to eat 15 different kinds of fruit on the 15th of Shevat. Try to buy dried fruits, nuts, and jaffa oranges grown in Israel for your celebration.

Session Plan

Gathering   Varies

Greet the children as they arrive and hand out stickers. Invite them to decorate the Jewish Calendar and the *Special Times* sign for the poster and hang the poster on the classroom door. Chat with them about trees by asking, "What do we get from trees?" Some responses might be fruit, nuts, wood, shade, places for birds and animals to live.

Focusing   10 minutes

When everyone has arrived, gather the group in a circle. After everyone is settled, show them the basket of fruits and nuts of Israel. Ask the children to name as many as they can, and fill in the names of any they do not know. Point out that all of them grow on trees. You may want to mention the shell that protects the fruit and the seed that will grow new fruit.

Conversation and Story   20 minutes

Read *The Man Who Planted Trees*.

Invite responses and comments about the story from the children.

Song — 5 minutes

Say, "Now let's stand up and sing a song called 'Standing Like a Tree.'" Sing the song two or three times.

Activity — Varies

There are four possible projects from which to choose. The timing for some will vary depending on your circumstances, so you may need to make adjustments in your schedule.

Creating a Plant Window

This activity should take about 10 minutes. Put potting soil in a small cup or pot. Plant the seeds according to directions in the seed catalog or on the packet. You might recruit an indoor gardener to help, or consult an indoor gardening book.

Tree Planting Outdoors

If arrangements have been made to do so, plant a tree outdoors.

Planting a Tree in Israel

If you decide to do this, you might use this time to plan with the children how to collect the necessary money (hold a bake sale after services, for example). You could also explain to the children how you will send the money to The Jewish National Fund and how they will use it.

Tree Walk

Take a tree walk in your church neighborhood or in a park. Identify trees by bark, leaf, fruit, and other identifying characteristics. Select a favorite tree and sit under it, hug it, or climb it (if it is safe to do so) to get to know it better.

Closing Circle — 5 minutes

Light the chalice candle and say something like, "What was the best part of our morning together?" Allow time for responses.

Close by saying, "We are grateful for trees that give us shade from the sun, hold water in the ground, grow food to eat and beautiful flowers and leaves to enjoy. May we plant trees for those who will come into the world after us. Shalom."

Evaluation and Planning

Who will water the seedling plants? Are they in a spot that is not too hot or cold? What follow up is needed?

What session will be used next week? What do you need to prepare?

Standing Like A Tree

Words & Music: Betsy Rose

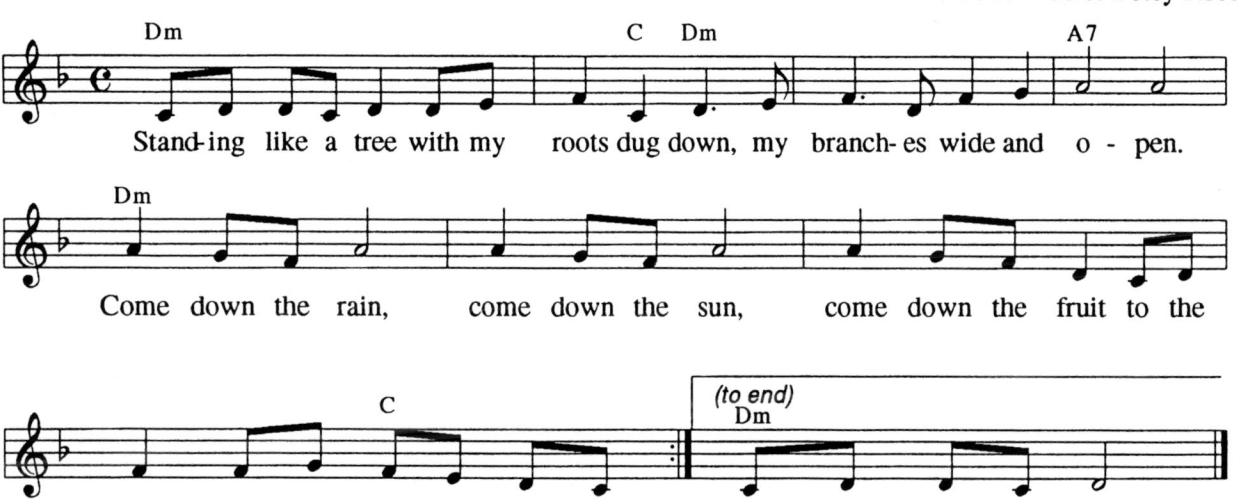

Standing like a tree with my roots dug down, my branches wide and open.
Come down the rain, come down the sun, come down the fruit to the heart that is open to be standing like a tree.

Session 15: A Time to Plant Trees

16 A Time to Say "I Love You"— Valentine's Day

Goals for Participants

- To explore concepts of love for family and friends.
- To express love for others.

Materials

- Copies of Resource 19, "Heart Patterns," for each participant
- Heart-shaped object, such as paperweight, soap, or large pendant
- Stickers of hearts
- Posterboard in red, pink, and white or paper plates
- Scissors
- Hole punch
- Pens and pencils
- Yarn
- White glue
- Chalice, candles, and matches
- For Craft Center: red, pink, and white construction paper; heart patterns; small paper doilies; valentine stickers
- Books about friends and friendship and the following titles for the Reading Corner:
  It's Valentine's Day, by Jack Prelutsky
  One Zillion Valentines, by Frank Modell
  Valentine Friends, by Ann Schweninger

Preparation

- Read through the entire session plan and decide who will lead each activity.

- Make a sign, "*Special Times* celebrates *St. Valentine's Day* today," for the Unitarian Universalist poster.

- Practice reading or telling "A Winter Day" for the Conversation and Story activity.

- Practice singing "Love is a Circle" and rehearse the dance steps for the Song activity. Prepare to teach it, or recruit a musician and/or song leader. Write the lyrics on newsprint or the chalkboard to help the children learn the words.

- To make valentine wreaths, cut out some rings from paper plates or posterboard. Make enough rings for each child and set aside for them to decorate. Or you can leave this activity for the children.

- Obtain all necessary materials for activities and Special Corners.

Background

The origins of Valentine's Day are lost in time, but at least two separate traditions are honored on this day devoted to love and lovers. In Ancient Rome, February 15th was the date of a festival honoring Juno, the goddess of women and marriage, and Pan, the god of nature. During this festival, birds and small animals were said to choose their mates. Following suit, young women put their names on slips of paper in a jar, and young men drew them out to choose sweethearts. Eventually, Roman soldiers carried this custom to England.

In 1415 the very first valentine card is said to have been sent by the Duke of Orleans who was imprisoned in the Tower of London. Valentine cards were made by hand for centuries, until 1809 when the first cards were printed and sold, starting a Victorian fad that continues today.

Valentine's Day is also the feast day of two martyred Christian saints. According to tradition, both of these Saint Valentines were executed on February 14, although in different years, and both have associations with love. One was a priest who lived in Rome during the third century. When he was jailed for aiding Christians, he was credited with curing his jailer's daughter of blindness. Other stories say that he fell in love with her. In either case, he is supposed to have written her a note thanking her for her kindness and signed it "From your Valentine." The second was a bishop of Terni who was martyred either for converting a Roman family to Christianity or for continuing to marry couples after the emperor forbade it.

In recent years, attempts have been made to shift the emphasis of this celebration to focus on prisoners, especially those who are imprisoned for political, religious, or ethnic reasons. If there is a group in your area which focuses on the children of prisoners, you may wish to organize a project around the class sending valentines and/or gifts to these children. Your local Amnesty International would be an excellent source of information for such a social service project.

Session Plan

Gathering   Varies

As the children arrive, greet them individually and hand out heart stickers to decorate the Christian Calendar and the *Special Times* sign for the poster. Hang the poster on the classroom door. Ask the children if they know what holiday is associated with hearts, then engage them in a conversation about how they celebrate Valentine's Day.

Focusing   10 minutes

Gather in a circle on chairs or on the rug. Pass around and talk about the heart-shaped object. Say something like, "No one knows exactly why the heart is connected with love, but we do use the heart as a symbol for love. Where do we see it used that way?" Allow time for responses.

Continue, "There are many ways to say 'I love you.' How many ways can we name?" Give some examples of how you show love and invite their responses.

Then say, "Today we'll hear a story about one family's way of saying 'I love you' by helping others. Then we'll sing a song and make a valentine wreath."

Conversation and Story   15 minutes

Read the story, "A Winter Day."

Engage the children in a conversation around some of these questions:

How would you feel if your father or mother asked you to give up your dinner to someone else who was hungry?

We all can't give away our dinners, but are there other ways we can help? If appropriate talk about the food basket in your church or about members in your congregation who help in a local soup kitchen.

In the story, Louisa entertains the children to keep their minds off the cold. What are some ways we can help in our homes?

Then say, "At Choices Time, you may want to make Valentine cards for some of your friends, or your mom or dad, or brother or sister. First, though, let's make Valentine wreaths, which we might call circles of love, and later we'll sing a song called, 'Love is a Circle.'"

Activity   15 minutes

Give each child a paper ring that you made earlier, or give them a paper plate and have them cut a circle out of the center. Punch one hole in the ring. Insert a short piece of yarn through the hole and secure it with a knot. Write the child's name on the back side of the ring.

Invite the children to cut enough hearts out of construction paper to completely cover their rings. Show them the heart patterns they can use. The hearts may be all one size or many sizes.

Spread a thin coating of glue over the front of the ring. Glue the hearts to the ring, overlapping as desired.

Engage the children in a discussion about

what they can do with their wreaths. They may want to keep and hang them in their room at home; give to a parent, brother, sister, or friend; hang up in the classroom; use to decorate the food basket at church; etc.

Choices Time   Varies

As the children finish making their Valentine wreaths, point out the choices available: materials for making valentines in the Craft Center, or books about Valentine's Day and friendship in the Reading Corner.

Song   10 minutes

Sing "Love is a Circle."
  Teach the movements as follows:

Stand in a circle with hands joined.
On the words, "round and round,"
  circle to the left.
On "love is up,"
  all lift hands.
On "love is down,"
  all stoop with hands toward floor.
On "love is inside,"
  all lean forward.
On "trying to get out,"
  lean backward.
On "whirling and twirling about,"
  release hands and whirl and twirl.
On the first part of the chorus,
  join hands and circle to the left, then to the right.
On "love is ours alone to give,"
  release and extend hands toward those opposite in the circle.
On "it lives in us,"
  touch chest with hands.
On "it's beautiful,"
  join hands again.

Continue through the other verses, fitting the movements to the words. For example, on "love will hide, love will show," cover and reveal faces; on "love is a laugh," laugh!

Closing Circle   5 minutes

At the conclusion of the song, sit in a circle where you are. Place the chalice candle in the center of the circle and light it.

Say something like, "On this Valentine's Day, may we know ourselves to be loved and loving. Let's celebrate this circle of love by naming each one of us and completing this sentence: 'We love (child's name) because (she has a beautiful smile).'"

Extinguish the candle.

Evaluation and Planning

What worked well? What could have been planned differently?

What session will be used next week? If your next session is Purim, Session 17, read through the entire session and remember to mail a letter (see Resource 20) to each participant.

A Winter Day

by Mary-Lib Whitney

Louisa was cold. She and her family huddled around a fire in the corner of their kitchen that was scarcely big enough to warm them. The wood pile was low, and they didn't know when they would be able to afford more. Mother kept the fire low to save wood.

They were poor, but Father loved his family and they had lots of fun together. Father always had a story to tell and often after supper he would tell story after story. Mother was always humming a tune as she worked. Louisa loved it when Mother sang her to sleep at night. So even when times were hard, they were happy. Once, they were so generous that they gave their own breakfast to a family that had no food.

A knock at the door took Father away from the fire. When he returned, he told them that a neighbor's child had come to ask for some wood; the baby was sick and they had no wood for their fire. Father asked his family to carry half their own wood to the neighbors.

"But we have a baby, too, and we don't have enough wood for ourselves," Mother complained.

"Wood will come," said Father, "or the storm will end." He set off for the neighbor's house, his arms full of wood.

Louisa played with the other children, and made up stories for them to keep them from thinking about the cold. The storm didn't get better, and they had just decided to go to bed early when a knock came at the door. It was a farmer from up the road with a load of wood that he was taking to sell in Boston. He had started out in his wagon, but the snowdrifts were so high that he couldn't get through. He asked if he could leave his wood at their house. "You can pay for it whenever you have the money," he said. Father had been right.

Louisa May Alcott grew up to write many stories and books. In one of them, *Little Women*, she tells of her experiences growing up in Concord, MA, and her family all became characters in her book.

Love Is a Circle

Words and Music: Phyllis Unger Hiller

1. Love is a cir-cle round and round, Love is up, Love is down, Love is in-side Trying to get out, Love is whirl-ing and twirling a-bout.

CHORUS:
Love is a cir-cle, it knows no bounds. The more you give the more comes a-round. Love is ours a-lone to give, It lives in us, it's beau-ti-ful.

2. Love is a circle trying to bend,
   Love is pieces trying to mend,
   Love is darkness waiting for light,
   Love is power and love is might.

3. Love is a laugh, love is a look,
   Love is the chance somebody took,
   Love will hide, love will show,
   The more you give, the more it grows.

4. Love is a circle, round and round,
   Love in the corners of squares can be found,
   Love is reaching, spreading its wings,
   Love will dance, and love will sing.

"Love Is a Circle": from the Children's Audiocassette Recording RAMO, A Song Story published by Oak Hill Music Publishing Co., P.O. Box 120068, Nashville, TN 37212. (615) 297-HOPE. Copyright © 1971 by Phyllis Unger Hiller.

17 A Time to Celebrate Victory Over Discrimination—Purim

Goals for Participants

- To learn the joy of times when the Jewish people have been saved from destruction.
- To consider the concept of discrimination.

Materials

- Copies of Resource 20, "Purim Letter to Participants," for each participant
- Stickers of Jewish star and other Purim related items
- Large appliance carton with the back removed
- Groggers (noisemakers)
- Construction paper or newspaper (14 x 22")
- Markers and crayons
- Glitter and glue
- Scissors
- Tape
- Paper clips
- Costumes of crowns, three cornered hats, masks, and robes
- Props for acting out the story: "lots" (slips of paper with dates), scrolls for proclamations, knobs for television carton, etc.
- Hamantaschen (three-cornered) cookies or other small treats
- Napkins
- Chalice, candle, and matches
- Books for the Reading Corner, such as:
  All About Jewish Holidays and Customs, by Morris Epstein
  Jewish Days and Holidays, by Greer Ray Cashman
  Jewish Holiday Fun, by Judith Hoffman Corwin
  Picture Book of Jewish Holidays, by David A. Adler
  My Very Own Megillah, by Judith Saypol and Madeline Wikler

Preparation

- Read through the entire session plan and decide who will lead each part of the session.

- Early in the week, photocopy Resource 20 and mail them to the children.

- Make a sign, "*Special Times* celebrates today *Purim,*" for the Unitarian Universalist poster.

- Make or purchase several groggers (noisemakers) from a Jewish supply shop, or transform Halloween or New Year's Eve noisemakers (not the simple shaker type) by painting them or covering them with tape.

- Use the patterns from Resource 21 to make Purim Crowns and Haman's Hats for the children to decorate. Cut out the crowns on gold construction paper.

- Practice reading "The Story of Purim" for the Conversation and Story activity.

- Plot out a rough outline of a television drama based on "The Story of Purim." The children can improvise for their performance, but things will go more smoothly if you plan based on your group and your space.

- Cut a large rectangle in the front of the appliance carton for the television.

- Bring a few treats for the Purim feast to add to the food some of the children may have brought.

- Obtain all necessary materials for activities and Special Corners.

Background

Purim has been described as one of the most festive of all Jewish holidays, a day of fun, good cheer, and merrymaking. It is a time for drama, for festivity, and for the giving of gifts (often ready-to-eat food).

Purim celebrates the victory of Esther and Mordechai over wicked Haman. The story is in the biblical Book of Esther, but not in the Torah, hence it is only of rabbinic origin. The name Purim means "lots," for Haman used a lot (*pur*) to decide when to kill the Jews. The day is celebrated with costumes, masquerades, plays, and parades. These activities are meant to make Purim a day when everything is topsy-turvy, upside-down.

The story in the Book of Esther is a tale of court intrigue. The story takes place in the ancient kingdom of Persia which spreads over 127 countries. King Ahasuerus is the rich and happy ruler. The stage is set with Queen Vashti being banished and Esther being chosen the new queen in a beauty contest. The courtier, Haman, becomes the chief advisor, but Mordechai, Esther's protector, refuses to bow down to him. Haman becomes very angry with all the Jews and convinces the King to sign a decree calling for the massacre of the Jews throughout the kingdom. Mordechai and Esther work to counteract the plan. Esther wines and dines the King, and then reveals that she is Jewish and pleads for her people. Haman is hanged and the Jews are saved. Mordechai and Esther hold a great feast to celebrate and live happily ever after.

The nature of the story has led to much debate among scholars who question its historical authenticity. But whether the story really happened or is pure fantasy, the Book of Esther and Purim have become accepted by the Jewish people as part of their festive cycle.

The lighthearted tone of the story and the Book of Esther deal also with an abiding serious issue for Jews living in Persia or any diaspora (Jews or Jewish communities living outside of Palestine or modern Israel). According to Edward Greenstein in *The Jewish Holidays, A Guide and Commentary*:

"Jews are unlike anyone else. They are a nation living among all the nations, with ways of their own, loyalties to each other and to their tradition, and yet asserting their loyalty to the nations in which they reside. Gentiles ask the question, 'How can Jews be loyal to their own nation and be loyal to ours?' The Book of Esther 'proves' that the Jews can. Mordechai saves the King from assassination and Esther is queen yet they remain Jews."

Since there is only one session on this topic, the emphasis is on merrymaking and festivity. But beneath the Purim celebration is the serious concern about discrimination against Jews and other minorities. Strive to help the children understand the meaning of discrimination as an unfavorable attitude or feeling about a person or group of people that is based on ignorance and/or misinformation. Children need concrete examples to understand this concept.

Session Plan

Gathering   Varies

Greet the children as they arrive. Give Purim stickers to each child to decorate the Jewish Calendar and the *Special Times* sign for the poster. Hang the poster on the classroom door. Show them the grogger (noisemaker) and let them take turns twirling it.

Focusing   5 minutes

Gather in a circle and say something like, "Today we are celebrating a Jewish holiday called Purim. This is one Jewish holiday when you might hear lots of noise (use the grogger and stamp your feet to demonstrate) even in the most solemn of synagogues.

"I'll tell you a story about Purim, and you'll see what I mean about noise."

Conversation and Story — 15 minutes

Say something like, "Discrimination is an unfavorable feeling about a person or group of people that is based on ignorance—not knowing that person—or on wrong information. One example is if I said to you, 'All people who wear glasses are dumb,' or 'Children are always noisy.' Can you think of some examples of discrimination?" Allow time for discussion.

Then continue, "Every year about this time, the Purim holiday celebrates a period when the Jews—although discriminated against—were saved from being destroyed. The Purim story, in the Hebrew Bible, is the story of Esther, Mordechai, and Haman."

Read "The Story of Purim" once, ignoring the instructions to make noise.

Say, "I will tell the story again. As I tell the story this time, I will need your help. Whenever I mention wicked Haman (make noise here), you need to stamp your feet to help me drown out his name." Practice this briefly with the children. Then tell the story again.

Activity — 10-15 minutes

Say, "It's traditional to act out the story of the Purim, so let's do a television drama. What parts do we need to fill? Who would like to be Haman (make noise here)? Esther? Mordechai? King Ahasuerus?"

Also include the role of an audience to stomp and shake the groggers during the performance! It may be possible for people to have roles and be part of the audience, too.

Invite the children to the craft table to make three-cornered hats and crowns and to finish the props—lots, scrolls, knobs for television carton.

Hand out costumes and props as needed. It is probably best to give each participant just a few lines, then you can read the story, cueing each player's line(s). For example, say, "Then Esther said to the King..." Or you can avoid lines and have the children pantomime the story as you read it.

The Performance — Varies

This will be a noisy, enthusiastic re-telling of the story.

Closing Circle — 10 minutes

Gather for a feast. Enjoy the cookies and other treats brought in by the children. Point out that the hamentaschen represents the three-cornered hat worn by Haman (much noise, of course!).

After the feast, light the chalice candle and say, "We celebrate the joy of that time long ago when the Jewish people were saved. Shalom."

Evaluation and Planning

What worked well?

Did issues arise (perhaps related to discrimination) which may need to be talked about later? What session will be used next week?

Plan ahead for the Lenten period before Easter. Consider possible projects—groups or agencies—to whom the children's contributions will be given. Your congregation may have policies in place regarding the collection of money for community projects. Be sure to check with the RE Committee, Board of Trustees, religious educator, or minister before finishing plans.

If your church school hasn't already participated in the Unitarian Universalist Service Committee's "Guest At Your Table" project, you may want to choose that as your project. You may order the boxes from the UUSC free of charge. Ask your director or minister of religious education to help with this.

If your next scsion is Lent, Session 18, read through the entire session and remember to mail a letter (see Resource 22) to each participant.

The Story of Purim

by Judith Hoffman Corwin

Long, long ago, the king of Persia was named Ahasuerus and the queen was Vashti. But she refused his latest command and he forced her to leave the country. Then the king issued a proclamation. There was to be a great beauty pageant. The most beautiful woman in the pageant would be the new queen. Eshter was named the new queen. The king did not know that she was Jewish.

One day, Esther's cousin, Mordechai, overheard two soldiers plotting to kill the king. Mordechai quickly told Esther, who informed the king. The story of how the king's life was saved was entered into the palace records.

The king's chief adviser was named Haman (make noise here). Haman (noise) was a wicked and proud man who expected everyone to bow down when he walked through the streets. But Mordechai would not bow before Haman (noise), since a Jew bows only to God. So Haman (noise) decided to kill not only Mordechai, but every Jew in Persia! To decide on the most favorable day for the slaughter, Haman (noise) cast lots, which is like picking a number from a hat when you play a game. The Hebrew word for lots is purim, which is how this holiday gets it name.

At first, Haman (noise) convinced the king to go along with his plans. But then the king learned of Mordechai's part in saving his life and he also listened to the pleas of Esther. She had first fasted—gone without food—for three days to pray for guidance and strength, and then she had told the king that if he were to kill all the Jews, then she must die too since she was Jewish.

And so, the king changed his mind, and decided to spare the Jews. He had the wicked Haman (noise) hanged, and made Mordechai his chief adviser.

Ever since then, Jews have observed Purim. The day before Purim is a day of fasting in memory of Esther's fast. The fast is followed by two days of dancing, merrymaking, feasting, and gladness.

Throughout history, Jewish families and communities have also celebrated private Purims when they were saved from great danger.

Copyright © 1987 by Judith Hoffman Corwin. Reprinted by permission of Julian Messner, A Division of Simon & Schuster, Inc.

18 A Time to Help Others—Lent

Goals for Participants

- To learn about the Christian practice of penitence and service which precedes Easter.
- To understand the importance of sharing what we have with others.
- To learn the story of Jesus feeding the multitudes and apply its meaning to life.
- To learn about the Unitarian Universalist Service Committee and the work it does around the world to help others.

Materials

- Copies of Resource 22, "Lenten Letter to Participants and Parents," for each participant
- Copies of Resource 23, "The Flaming Chalice Symbol," for each participant
- Stickers of bread, fish, and baskets
- Picture of hungry and/or homeless people
- Unitarian Universalist Service Committee "Guest at Your Table" boxes
- Posterboard or cardboard
- Scissors
- Red construction paper
- Pens, pencils, and markers
- White glue
- Chalice, candle, and matches
- Books for the Reading Corner, such as:
  A Rose for Abby, by Donna Guthrie (This book shows homeless and hungry people with illustrations of children helping.)
  The Miracles of Jesus, *The Parables of Jesus*, and *Book of Bible Stories, New International Version*, all by Tomie de Paolo
  Easter, by Gail Gibbons

Preparation

- Read through the entire session plan and decide who will lead each activity.

- Early in the week, make copies of Resource 22 and mail them to each participant.

- Make a sign "*Special Times* celebrates *Lent* today" for the Unitarian Universalist poster.

- Decide on your Lenten project. If you are going to do the Unitarian Universalist Service Committee "Guest at Your Table" project, order boxes and information from the Unitarian Universalist Service Committee, 130 Prospect St., Cambridge, MA 02139; (617) 868-6600. Order enough boxes for each child and prepare a brief explanation of the project.

- Prepare to read or tell the stories: "Loaves and Fishes" and "The Flaming Chalice."

- Obtain all necessary materials for activities and Special Corners.

Background

Lent is a period of time observed by Christians as preparation for Easter celebrations. Traditionally it is associated with penitence and fasting, prayer and service.

In the second century Christians observed a rigorous fast for 40 hours, from the afternoon of Good Friday (the day of the crucifixion) to Easter morning. This period of fasting was lengthened in the fourth century by the Christian Church, which decreed the 40 day period of Lent—from Ash Wednesday to Easter. Members were expected to abstain from worldly pleasures and certain foods. This dimension was added to commemorate the 40 days and 40 nights that Jesus fasted in the wilderness in preparation for his ministry. Modern Christian practices of prayer meetings and inter-church services are designed for religious growth and renewal, contemplation and self-improvement.

Lent begins on Ash Wednesday, a day set aside to attend church and confess one's sins in preparation for the holy season. In Roman Catholic churches, the ashes of burned palm branches from the previous year's celebrations of Palm Sunday are placed on the foreheads of worshippers in the sign of the cross. This is a sign of penitence.

For Unitarian Universalists, Lent offers us an excellent opportunity to tell the story of Easter and to do things in service of others. Children will want to know the meaning of Ash Wednesday, Good Friday, the crucifixion, and the resurrection. Here is one explanation from a pamphlet on Easter written by the UUA's Department of Religious Education.

A certain teacher named Jesus, who went from place to place to talk to people about life, about getting along with other people, and about other important things, was much loved by some but greatly mistrusted and even feared by others. Once, as he went to the city to celebrate a holy day, his friends greeted him with cheers and affection but his enemies invented excuses to have him arrested, convicted of breaking the laws, and sentenced to be killed. His friends were helpless to prevent this, and Jesus was hanged on a cross until he died, which was the way men were executed in those days.

The next morning some of his friends went to the tomb where his body had been taken and found it was not there. No one knew then or knows now just what did happen. Perhaps his friends moved his body and dared not say that they had. Some believe, however, that through a miracle Jesus came back to life. Some believed it so sincerely that they were sure that they saw him and could hear his voice. Many Christians still believe in the literal resurrection of Christ's body. Others, believing in immortality, interpret the resurrection story as symbolically affirming the continuing life, not of Jesus' body, but of his spirit or soul. Some of us believe that it was his ideas, his teachings, his love for people and their love for him which could not be killed.

This session includes a service project—the Unitarian Universalist Service Committee "Guest at Your Table" or one of your choice.

Session Plan

Gathering   Varies

As the children arrive, greet them individually and hand out stickers. Ask the children what the stickers remind them of and then decorate the Christian Calendar and the *Special Times* sign for the poster. Hang the poster on the classroom door.

Focusing   10 minutes

Gather in a circle in chairs or on a rug. Show the group pictures of hungry or homeless people. Ask, "What do you think these pictures show?" Allow time for responses.

Then say something like, "Today, we will learn more about Lent, the time of almost six weeks before Easter when Christians think about Jesus and the power of love through the stories he taught and the life he led."

Conversation and Story   15 minutes

Say, "The story we are going to hear today is called a miracle story. Something happens in this story that we cannot explain because it does not seem that it could really have happened. Some people say only Jesus could make it happen. Others say it is a story of many people sharing what food they had so that all could eat. The story is from the Book of John in the Bible."

Read the story, "The Loaves and the Fishes."

After the story, engage the children in conversation around these questions: "What do you think really happened? What is a miracle? Let's name some every day miracles. Let's talk about a way we can help make a miracle happen through the Unitarian Universalist Service Committee."

Activity   20 minutes

Say, "One of the ways we can share what we have with others during Lent is to save our pennies and nickels and dimes and give them to the Unitarian Universalist Service Committee.

"To help us collect and save the money we will give to the UUSC, we have Unitarian Universalist Service Committee boxes to take home with us."

From the UUSC literature, tell the stories behind the people's faces on the four sides of the "Guest at Your Table" boxes.

Tell the story of the Unitarian Universalist Service Committee flaming chalice, which can be found at the end of this session.

Choices Time   Varies

Point out the available choices: Reading Corner and the Craft Center to make a flaming chalice poster. For the flaming chalice poster, hand out copies of Resource 23. The children can cut out the flaming chalice symbol and glue it to posterboard. Or they can draw their own flaming chalice symbol on red construction paper, cut it out, and glue it to posterboard.

Closing Circle   5 minutes

Light the chalice candle and say something like, "We light this candle for Jesus who taught us that by helping others we help ourselves. We light this chalice for the Unitarian Universalist Service Committee who has been helping people around the world for 50 years. Let's welcome guests at our tables and make our circle of friends grow. Go in peace."

Give a box to each child to take home.

Evaluation and Planning

What worked well? What could have been done differently? How will you follow up on the Lenten offering? Can you get "Guest At Your Table" boxes to any of the children who were absent today?

Are there ways to link the next session with this one?

The Loaves and the Fishes

Often Jesus would preach or speak to large crowds of people. Once when a large group had gathered to hear him, Jesus said to his followers, "How will we feed all these people? Where are we to buy bread for these people to eat? Are there people in the crowd who have food?'"

And one of his friends, Andrew, said, "There is a boy here who has food. He has five loaves of barley bread and two fish. But what are they among so many people?"

"Have the people sit down," said Jesus, "and bring the boy and his loaves and fishes to me." The people sat down on the grass, about five thousand in all.

When they did so, Jesus took the loaves and the fish and, when he had given thanks, began to distribute them to the people.

Soon all had had enough to eat, and Jesus said, "Gather up what is left for us to give to the poor, so that nothing will be wasted."

And his helpers did so, and they filled twelve baskets.

The Flaming Chalice: Symbol of Unitarian Universalism

The Flaming Chalice in a circle is the symbol of Unitarian Universalism. The flaming chalice is a flame burning the holy oil of helpfulness and sacrifice—spreading warmth and light and hope. The circle in which it is contained represents our Unitarian and Universalist heritage with its concept of world-wide community.

The chalice has been a symbol of liberal religion since the 15th century, dating back to John Hus in Transylvania. The flaming chalice was adopted by the Unitarian Service Committee in 1941. Its current story is an interesting one.

Hans Deutsch was an Austrian refugee who lived in Paris until France was invaded in 1940. He had worked in many European countries as a musician, draftsman, and portrait artist. Having contributed many cartoons of unflattering contents (concerning Hitlerism) to several papers in Vienna, he fled Paris and finally settled in Portugal. To earn a living he gave lessons in English, one of the eight languages he spoke, and drew portraits.

It was in Portugal that Deutsch joined the staff of the Unitarian Service Committee for a period of six months as secretary and assistant to Dr. Charles E. Joy, then the Executive Director of USC.

Dr. Joy asked his new assistant to work in his spare time on a symbol for the Committee. The Flaming Chalice was created in response to this request and given to the Committee by Deutsch in appreciation of its humanitarian work.

When Hans Deutsch was threatened with imprisonment in Portugal in June 1941, the USC assisted him in escaping to the United States where he now resides as John H. Derrick.

Recently, the chalice has been redesigned and made the official symbol of the Unitarian Universalist Association of Congregations.

19 A Time to Be Free from Slavery—Pesah

Goals for Participants

- To learn about the meaning of freedom to the Jews.
- To celebrate the Jewish Passover—a festival of spring and a commemoration of the exodus of the Jews from Egypt.
- To enjoy the experience of preparing a special feast together.

Materials

- Four copies of Resource 24, "The Four Questions," for adults who will read the responses
- Seder plate with symbolic foods, or an illustrated Seder plate
- Stickers of eggs, Seder designs, and Jewish stars
- Ingredients for matzoh and haroset (see recipes at the end of the session)
- Utensils for food preparation (see recipes at the end of the session)
- Grape juice
- Paper plates, cups, plastic spoons
- 3 x 5" cards
- Chalice, candle, and matches
- Books for the Reading Corner, such as:
  Festival of Freedom: The Story of Passover, re-told by Maida Silverman
  The Four Questions, by Lynne Sharon Schwartz
  Jewish Days and Holidays, by Greer Fay Cashman
  Jewish Holiday Fun, by Judith Hoffman Corwin
  My Very Own Haggadah, by Judith Saypol and Madeline Wikler
  Passover, A Season of Freedom, by Malka Drucker
  A Picture Book of Passover, by David A. Adler

Preparation

- Read through the entire session plan and decide who will lead each part.

- Make a sign "*Special Times* celebrates *Pesah* today" for the Unitarian Universalist poster.

- Recruit additional adult assistance for the Seder meal and/or music as needed.

- Obtain the ingredients to make matzoh and haroset. You may want to purchase matzoh due to time constraints. If you choose to make it, you will need access to an oven. If using a portable oven in the classroom, experiment at home first.

- Collect materials and prepare a Seder plate with some or all of the symbolic foods: lamb bone, egg, salt water, parsley, bitter herb (horseradish), and grape juice. Or purchase an illustrated Seder plate in a card shop or Jewish goods store. You could also find an illustration in a book and copy it onto a paper plate, using colored markers to illustrate the foods.

- Practice singing the "Dayenu" chorus for the Conversation and Story activity. Write out the lyrics on newsprint or chalkboard to help the children learn the words.

- Prepare to tell or read the story, "A Free People."

- Print the four questions from Resource 24 on 3 x 5" cards, one question per card.

- If possible, plan to serve the Seder meal with the children sitting around low tables like coffee tables, or sitting around a cloth on the floor.

- Obtain all necessary materials for activities and Special Corners.

Background

Passover (Pesah) is an ancient Jewish festival which celebrates the Exodus of the Hebrew people from slavery and oppression in Egypt. The name Passover is taken from the Exodus story found in the Hebrew scriptures in the Book of Exodus: "During the tenth and final plague inflicted on Pharaoh to break his will, God passed over the Jews and struck down only the Egyptian firstborn." It was that night that the pharaoh finally agreed to let the Jewish people go. Ever since then, Jews gather together on that night to commemorate and contemplate the meaning of freedom.

The central meaning of Pesah is liberation—from slavery to freedom—and so is called the "season of our liberation." But Pesah has another name—the holiday of spring—celebrating the liberation of the earth from the grip of winter. Therefore, the holiday of liberation is the holiday of spring with the themes of hope and rebirth. Pesah proclaims the possibilities of liberation and renewal, reminding us that freedom is as intrinsic to human nature as blossoming trees is to the natural world.

After the destruction of the Temple, Pesah became a home festival, its observance kept alive through the generations even under great oppression and persecution. The last supper shared by Jesus and his disciples was a Passover Seder (ritual meal). When appropriate, either at Passover and/or Easter, tie the Jewish and Christian scriptures together recognizing the source of the Christian mass and communion service with the Jewish Seder. In contemporary Judaism, Passover is sometimes celebrated in community Seders.

Many Unitarian Universalist churches (and many Christian churches) now observe Passover with a Seder. Through participation in an age-old tradition, we connect with our Jewish heritage. Although there are Jews who believe it really happened as it is written in Exodus, there are others who believe that some parts of the story are true and some are not. There are some Jews who say they cannot believe in a God who would kill the first-born child of every Egyptian family or break the laws of nature to save certain people. But no matter what the many beliefs are about the story, this is a celebration which speaks to all who value freedom.

Pesah acknowledges the universal human yearning for freedom and expresses compassion for all the people in the world who are not free. The Seder is a time of hope and gratitude celebrated with family and friends. It is a time for each person to rededicate themselves to the cause of liberty and justice.

Session Plan

Gathering   Varies

Greet the children as they arrive, hand out stickers, and ask them to decorate the Jewish Calendar and the *Special Times* sign for the poster. Hang the poster on the classroom door. Invite them to look at the books in the Reading Corner, especially those with stories and pictures of Passover.

Focusing   5 minutes

Gather in a circle. Show the Seder plate and talk briefly about the five symbolic foods shown—horseradish for the bitterness of slavery, haroset for the mortar of brickmaking, shank bone for the sacrificial lamb, egg for new life, parsley for spring. Say, "This special plate is used during the celebration of the Jewish holiday of Passover. The Passover celebration includes a shared meal, called a Seder, and this is called a Seder plate. We will learn more about Passover through our activities this morning, but maybe you know something about it already." Allow time for responses.

Conversation and Song   10 minutes

Say, "Each spring, the Jewish people celebrate the festival of Passover. This celebrates the time the Jewish people escaped from being slaves in Egypt long, long ago. Do you know what being a slave means?" Take time to find out what the children think about slavery. Ask them about Harriet Tubman, Martin Luther King, Jr., Rosa Parks, or Malcolm X.

Go on to say, "We will hear pieces of the Passover story of the Jews as we go through the morning. In the Haggadah is the story and the meaning of the religious symbols. We will read from a Unitarian Universalist version of it. First, let's listen to the words and then sing the chorus of a song that tells part of the story. The song is called 'Dayenu' or 'It would have been enough.' It was a man called Moses who led the Jewish people out of Egypt, but in this song 'He' means God."

The musician should sing or the leader read the words of each verse and children sing the chorus "Dayenu" after each verse.

Activity   20 minutes

Say, "Now let's make some of the foods used in the Passover Seder." Both activities may be done simultaneously, if you have sufficient adult assistance. Involve the children in making the foods.

If the children lose interest in the food preparation, or to give others an opportunity to help with the preparation, an assistant can invite them to set up the Seder table with cups, plates, Seder plate in center, and so on.

Story and the Seder Meal   10-15 minutes

As soon as the food is ready, gather around the table or cloth on floor and tell the story of Moses and the Hebrews at the end of this session.

Read the story, "A Free People."

After the story, choose four children to read the four questions during the Seder meal and give them the question cards. Traditionally, the youngest child asks the first question, then the next youngest, and so on. Since the children's reading ability will vary, give the questions to those whom you know will be able to read them with comparative ease. You and other adults present will respond. Give a copy of Resource 24 to each of them.

Point again to the symbolic foods on the Seder plate and remind them of their significance—the lamb bone reminds us of the lamb the Hebrews killed to mark their doorposts with its blood; the haroset reminds us of the bricks they had to make for the pharaoh; the salt water reminds us of the tears shed by the Hebrew slaves; and the matzoh reminds us of the bread that did not have time to rise before they escaped.

Say to the children, "After the first question and answer is given, we will eat a small piece of matzoh and take a sip of grape juice. We'll eat the rest of our matzoh, the haroset, and drink our grape juice at the end."

Enjoy your Seder meal.

Closing Circle   5 minutes

Light the chalice candle and sing "Dayenu" chorus again.

Close by saying, "At this special time of the Jewish Passover, we give thanks for our freedom. Shalom."

Evaluation and Planning

Did things go as planned? What suggestions would you make for next year's leaders if they use this plan?

If Palm Sunday and Easter sessions are yet to come, plan to relate them to this session as appropriate.

Recipes for a Seder Meal

Making Matzoh

If you have time and the necessary equipment, this recipe is fun and easy to put together. Explain to the children that matzoh is unleavened bread, that it has no yeast, baking powder, or soda to make it rise, so when it's baked, it stays flat.

Ingredients
3 cups flour
1 1/2 cups water
extra flour to knead the dough

Utensils
large mixing bowl
measuring cups
rolling pin
fork
cookie sheet

Turn on the oven to 450°. Put the flour in a large mixing bowl and gradually add the water. Begin to knead the dough with your hands, adding extra flour if necessary, until you get a pliable mound of dough.

Divide the dough into eight balls; roll each of these into a circle and make into a piece of matzoh. Using a fork, make rows of holes in each of the matzohs in a neat pattern. Place the matzoh on the cookie sheet and bake for about 10-15 minutes, or until lightly browned. Makes 8 matzoh.

Copyright © 1987 by Judith Hoffman Corwin. Reprinted by permission of Julian Messner, A Division of Simon & Schuster, Inc.

Making Haroset
3 apples, peeled, cored, and chopped
1/2 cup grape juice
1/2 teaspoon powdered cinnamon
3/4 cup chopped almonds or walnuts

Mix apples with grape juice and cinnamon, mashing slightly with a fork. Add nuts and blend well. Add a few spoonfuls of liquid, if needed. Store in refrigerator.

Copyright © 1988 by Maida Silverman. Reprinted by permission of Simon & Schuster, Inc.

Dayenu

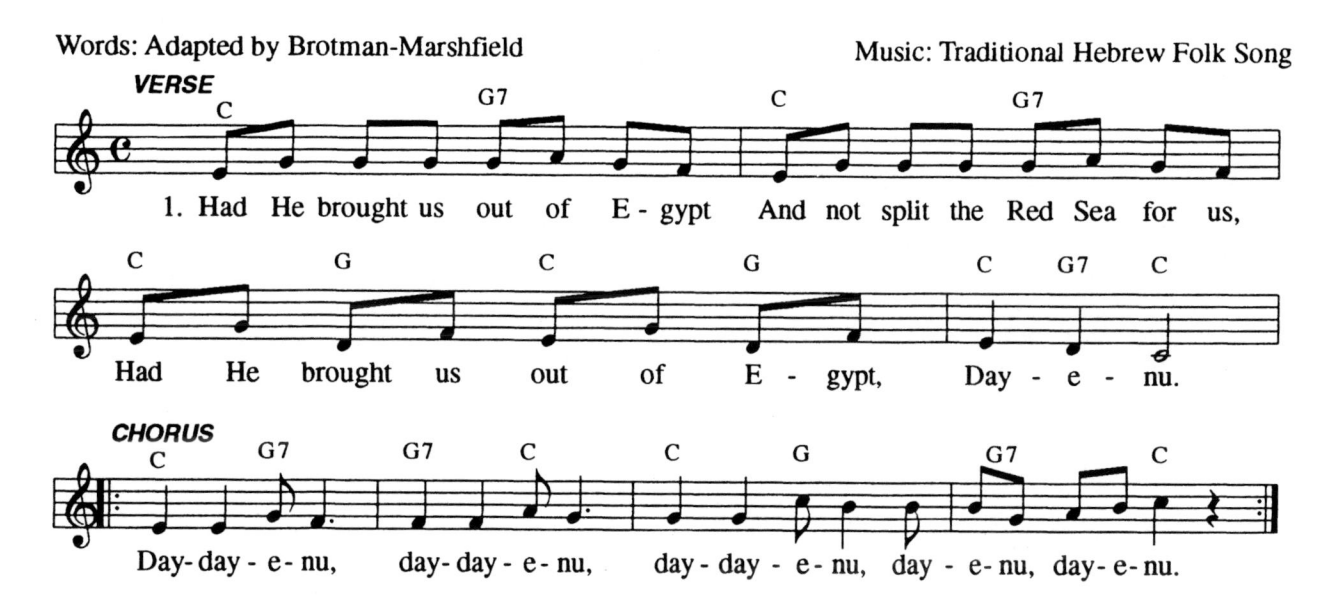

Words: Adapted by Brotman-Marshfield
Music: Traditional Hebrew Folk Song

[Verse musical notation with lyrics:]
1. Had He brought us out of E-gypt And not split the Red Sea for us, Had He brought us out of E-gypt, Day-e-nu.

[Chorus musical notation with lyrics:]
Day-day-e-nu, day-day-e-nu, day-day-e-nu, day-e-nu, day-e-nu.

2. Had He split the Red Sea for us
   And not brought us through dry shod
   Had He split the Red Sea for us, Dayenu.
   CHORUS

3. Had He fed us with mana
   And not given us the Sabbath,
   Had He fed us with mana, Dayenu.
   CHORUS

4. Had He given us the Sabbath
   And not brought us to Mount Sinai,
   Had He given us the Sabbath, Dayenu.
   CHORUS

5. Had He brought us to Mount Sinai
   And not given us the Torah,
   Had He brought us to Mount Sinai, Dayenu.
   CHORUS

6. Had He given us the Torah
   And not brought us to Israel,
   Had He given us the Torah, Dayenu.
   CHORUS

Session 19: A Time to Be Free from Slavery

A Free People

Long, long ago, the Hebrew people were slaves in Egypt. They were forced to make bricks out of straw and mud for the Egyptian Pharaoh (the king) for the large pyramids and monuments he was building. They worked hard and long and the pharaoh's soldiers were very cruel to them. A man called Moses heard a voice speak to him from a burning bush. The voice told him to go to the pharaoh and tell him that God said he was to free the Hebrews and let them leave Egypt.

Many times, Moses went to the pharaoh. Every time, the pharaoh said the Hebrews could leave. And every time, he went back on his word. Many plagues—storms, blood, hailstones, frogs, wild animals—befell the Egyptians and with each plague, the pharaoh said the Hebrews could leave. Then when the storm or the terrible happening was over, he changed his mind again.

Finally, Moses told the pharaoh that if he did not let the Hebrews go, a tenth plague would happen to the Egyptians and it would be the worst of all. An angel of death would come and kill all the first-born children of the Egyptians. The pharaoh was frightened and said that the Hebrews could leave Egypt.

Moses told the Hebrews to kill a lamb and paint some of its blood on the doorposts of their homes. When the Angel of Death came, it would pass over the homes whose doorposts were painted with blood and their children would not be killed. The Hebrews began to make bread for their journey, but before the bread had time to rise, they started off, for they were afraid the pharaoh would change his mind again and not let them go.

All of the Hebrews followed Moses. They walked to the edge of the Red Sea, and there a great miracle happened. The waters spread apart so that the Hebrews could pass through to the other side. The pharaoh did change his mind, and sent his soldiers after them. But when the soldiers reached the sea, the waters closed over again. The Hebrews were safe! They sang songs of joy. They were free once again! Many years later, the Hebrews came to be called Jews.

Each year the Jews celebrate the holiday of Passover to remember the time when they became a free people. This is the special ceremony of the Passover Seder.

20 A Time for the Teachings of Jesus—Palm Sunday

Goals for Participants

- To understand the meanings of Jesus' message of love.
- To become familiar with the events in Jesus' life leading up to his arrival in Jerusalem, and the beginning of Holy Week.

Materials

- Copies of Resource 25, "The Lord's Prayer," for each participant
- Stickers of palms and donkeys
- Gold cover stock or construction paper
- Pencils, pens, and fine-line black markers
- Scissors and glue
- Cassette player
- Taped music from *Jesus Christ, Superstar* or *Godspell*
- Chalice, candles, and matches
- Bible storybooks for the Reading Corner, such as:
  Miracles of Jesus, by Tomie de Paolo
  The Parables of Jesus, by Tomie de Paolo
  Easter, by Gail Gibbons

Preparation

- Read through the entire session plan and decide who will lead each activity. Decide if you will be using "The Golden Rule" or "The Lord's Prayer" activity.

- Make a sign "*Special Times* celebrates *Palm Sunday* today" for the Unitarian Universalist poster.

- Look for pictures of Jesus' entry into Jerusalem, showing the people waving palm branches in Bible storybooks.

- Find a copy of "The Golden Rule" in the Bible and print it on posterboard if you plan to use it for the Conversation and Story activity.

- Print on posterboard both versions of "The Lord's Prayer" from Resource 25, if you plan to use it for the Conversation and Story activity.

- Prepare to tell or read the story, "A Hosanna Day."

- Purchase a palm branch from a local florist or garden center. You can break off fronds from it for each child.

- Obtain all necessary materials for activities and Special Corners.

Background

Palm Sunday begins the Christian Holy Week, which commemorates the last week of Jesus' life. Several different versions of this important story are recounted in the New Testament (Matthew 21:1-9, Mark 11:1-10, Luke 19:28-38). When presenting this story to children, you will want to remind them that this is indeed a story.

Palm Sunday is a celebration of the events associated with the day when Jesus entered Jerusalem, enacting the Coming of the Messiah according to the Jewish traditions. His disciples took branches from the palm trees and placed them on the road ahead of him as he rode in on a donkey. Thus, the name Palm Sunday, a day of joy and triumph. In the seventh or eighth century, the Christian churches started the practice of blessing and distributing palm branches, which is continued in many Christian churches today.

Other events of Holy Week include Maundy (Holy) Thursday and Good Friday. Celebrations are held on Holy Thursday commemorating that day when Jesus washed the feet of his twelve friends (disciples) as he gathered with them for his last supper. The Friday before Easter commemorates the day Jesus was crucified. It is called "good" because Christians believe that Jesus atoned for the sins of the world through his death and was victorious over death.

In celebrating Palm Sunday, focus on the courage of Jesus who chose to come to Jerusalem and speak out about what he held sacred. It is important to reflect on the teachings of Jesus—the right relationship of one human being to another and of each person to her or his God, as exemplified in "The Lord's Prayer" and in "The Golden Rule." Choose one or both of these teachings to share with the children and make it a Hosanna day.

The teachings of Jesus emphasized in this session are found in the Christian scriptures: The Golden Rule is in Matthew 7:12 and Luke 6:31; The New Commandment is in Matthew 22:34-40, Mark 12:28-34, and Luke 10:25-28; and The Lord's Prayer is in Matthew 6:9-15.

Unitarian Universalist interpretations of these teachings can be found in *From Long Ago and Many Lands*, edited by Sophia Lyon Fahs, and "The Lord's Prayer," words by the Rev. Barbara Marshman.

Session Plan

Gathering   Varies

Greet the children as they arrive and hand out stickers to decorate the Christian Calendar and the *Special Times* sign on the the poster. Hang the poster on the classroom door. Invite them to browse through the books in the Book Corner, particularly those that have to do with Easter and the teachings of Jesus and/or listen to the music of *Jesus Christ, Superstar* or *Godspell*.

Focusing   10 minutes

Gather in a circle in chairs or on a rug. Show the illustration of Jesus entering Jerusalem. Say, "When Jesus and his friends came into Jerusalem, the people waved palm branches and shouted their welcome to Jesus. Why do you think they were so excited to see him?" Allow time for responses. Evoke from the children whatever they know about the event. If you have had the session on Lent, remind them of that session and of the Christmas story for background.

Conversation and Story   25 minutes

Say something like, "Because of the things that Jesus said and did, many people believed he was the 'messiah,' the one who would save the Jews from those who treated them unjustly and unfairly.

"Today we'll talk a little about some of the teachings that Jesus taught and then we will hear a Hosanna story.

"When Jesus was asked what the greatest commandment or law was, he answered, 'You should love God with all your heart, with all your soul, with all your mind!' He also added a new commandment: 'You shall love your neighbor as yourself.' What could he have meant by that?" Allow time for responses.

Then say, "Another of Jesus' teachings is called The Golden Rule—'Always treat others the way you would like them to treat you.'"

Ask, "Why is that a good rule? Would it be nice if everyone followed it?" Allow time for responses.

Then continue, "Jesus taught his friends—disciples—to pray 'The Lord's Prayer.'" Read the two versions of "The Lord's Prayer" that you wrote on posterboard, pausing after each line. Or read "The Golden Rule" if that is what you've chosen. If you read "The Lord's Prayer," engage the children in a conversation about the following phrases:

"who art in heaven"   life according to God's will—the greatest good

"our daily bread"   basic human needs of the community

96   *Special Times*

"forgive us our trespasses"	forgiveness and repentance
"the kingdom and the power and the glory forever"	community of love and justice (kindness and fairness)
"amen"	may it be so

Say, "Here is a special Palm Sunday story about a child your age."

Read the story, "A Hosanna Day."

Activity   15 minutes

Give the children their copies of "The Lord's Prayer" or point to "The Golden Rule." Invite them to illustrate some of the words and to highlight some of the phrases or scripture. Mount the finished pictures on gold construction or scroll paper for the children to take home.

Closing Circle   5 minutes

Gather in a circle. Light the chalice candle and say, "On this Palm Sunday, let us remember the teaching of Jesus, 'always treat others as you would like others to treat you.' Amen."

Break off fronds from a palm branch and give them to each child.

Evaluation and Planning

Have you set the stage for other events to come? If you do not meet on Easter Sunday, you may want to do Session 21, "A Time for Rebirth—Easter," on the following Sunday.

A Hosanna Day

by Mary-Lib Whitney

"Hosanna, hosanna," said Simcha over and over again. She loved the sound of the word and it made her feel good inside to say it. It was such a happy word. "Hosanna, praise God, hosannnaaaaaa." She tried saying it all different ways.

It was a beautiful day—not a cloud in the sky. She knew it would be hot later, but right now, as the sun came up, it was cool and the earth smelled sweet. She was going to Jerusalem with her family to spend Passover with her favorite aunt and uncle. It would be a long walk, and they would have to leave soon so that they could be there before the heat of early afternoon. She remembered the narrow streets that wound through the city and she thought of how cool her aunt's house would be. Her mother climbed onto the donkey and took the baby in her arms. Father held the donkey's halter as they walked along. Simcha danced and skipped all around the donkey, kicking up clouds of dust.

"Hold on there, young lady," said Father, laughing. "You'll have us all choking in dust and you'll be too worn out to make it all the way to the city."

Simcha calmed down. Her parents were talking grown-up talk, so she stopped listening. "I wonder if we will see Jesus," she thought. She had heard about Jesus. He was a great storyteller—she loved to listen to stories. She had heard that he was a kind person who cared about people who were poor or sick. He wanted to help people and make their lives better. He loved children, too. Maybe if she saw him he would tell her a story. "Hosanna, praise God," she whispered quietly to a bird sitting along the road, and the bird sang a song to her that Simcha thought sounded like "hosanna." Simcha was so happy. She felt as though she could dance all the way to Jerusalem.

As they got closer to the city, there were more and more people. Everyone who could, went to Jerusalem for Passover. She was glad she had people to stay with, because she knew the city would be very crowded. Many people would have to sleep on the ground outside the walls.

Suddenly, everyone seemed to be shouting. Simcha stretched her neck to see over the crowd. People were moving back to make a path leading up to the gate of the city. Simcha ducked under the arms of some grown-ups and found herself right at the edge of the path. It was dry and dusty. Passing feet stirred up little puffs of dust that made her sneeze. Everyone was shouting, "Hosanna." They had pulled branches off the palm trees and were waving them to cool themselves in the hot sun. Simcha thought someone very important must be coming. It couldn't be Romans because everyone was shouting "Hosanna" and that was such a happy word. The Romans were mean and made everyone sad.

Then she saw the man on the white donkey coming up the road. He was an ordinary looking man, but something special seemed to glow in his face. As he got closer, she saw his eyes. They seemed so very sad. She wanted to make him happy. She saw the donkey's feet kicking up dust and she was afraid it would make him sneeze, too. She took off her cloak and spread it on the path in front of him. Others saw her, and soon everyone was spreading their cloaks on the road, too. As the donkeys came closer to her, the man turned to her and smiled. He stopped the donkey and reached out his hand to touch her head. "Thank you," he said. His voice made her feel warm inside.

"Come, Jesus, we will be late," said the man holding the donkey's reins.

"In good time," said Jesus. "This child has been very kind to me. It is always the children who must teach us. It was a little boy who shared his meal so that I could feed the five thousand who had come to hear me. When a child shares, the whole world seems to follow. The prophet said, 'A little child shall lead them.' We have seen that here today. If we could all be as children, the world would be a better place."

Just then, Simcha's mother and father caught up to her and saw what had happened. How proud they were of their daughter.

Jesus rode on into the city. Simcha picked up her cloak, folded it carefully, and held it against her cheek. "Hosanna," she thought. "This has truly been a 'Praise God' day. Hurray for Jesus!"

21 A Time for Rebirth—Easter

Goals for Participants

- To learn the traditional story of Easter.
- To explore the meanings of that story.
- To think about experiences of rebirth and renewal during our lifetime.

Materials

- Copies of Resource 26, "Easter Symbols," for each participant
- Stickers of flowers and crosses
- Small basket for each child
- *Jesus Christ, Superstar* or *Godspell* cassette tapes
- Cassette player
- Tissue paper in a variety of colors
- Sand and Easter grass
- Palm branches
- Scissors and glue
- Popsicle sticks
- Cross or crucifix and pictures of cross and crucifixion
- Chalice, candle, and matches
- Books for Reading Corner, such as:
  Easter, by Gail Gibbons
  Book of Bible Stories, by Tomie de Paola

Preparation

- Read through the entire session plan and decide who will lead each activity.

- Make a sign "*Special Times* celebrates *Easter* today" for the Unitarian Universalist poster.

- Decide if you will read "The Origins of Easter" at the end of this session, or another story about Easter for the Conversation and Story activity.

- Learn the song "Alleluia Sing" and be prepared to teach it to the children or recruit a musician to sing with the children. If necessary, write the lyrics on newsprint or the chalkboard to help the children learn the words.

- Prepare a symbol basket with the appropriate Easter symbols arranged in it. To make the Easter symbols, photocopy Resource 26, cut out the Alleluia sunrise and Hosanna palm, and glue them to popsicle sticks. Make a cross out of two popsicle sticks, and include flowers and palm branches.

- Bring in spring flowers.

- Bring in an Easter snack of your choice for the whole class.

- Obtain all necessary materials for activities and Special Corners.

Background

This session focuses on the most important theological concepts in Christianity—the crucifixion and the resurrection. For almost 2,000 years people have struggled to understand their significance. The most common interpretation of the crucifixion and resurrection is that Jesus died on the cross as a sacrifice for the sins of humanity, so that individuals might experience the saving grace of God and his living presence in their midst. This is a very difficult concept for first and second graders, and it may not represent the views of their parents or their Unitarian Universalist congregation. The story in this session is condensed in narrative form without seeking to interpret the meaning of the events.

Though our children have heard the story of Jesus' birth and some of his teachings, this may be the first time the death of Jesus and the miracle of his victory over death have been addressed with them directly. It is a rich and meaningful story on many levels, and children will need time to talk about it and ask their own questions.

Although death has been addressed before in this program (All Souls' Day), the focus on death is more intense in this session. It is Jesus who is being put to death, and the children may recognize that this is a very important story about an important person.

As children listen to today's story, it is possible that some personal sorrow may be evoked, such as the death of a significant person in a child's life. Reassure children that sad feelings are an important part of our lives—that no one goes through life without some sorrow. Reassure them also that there are adults who care about them and who can help them through the painful times. If any child seems to need special attention, be sure to alert a parent, your minister, or your religious educator, so that additional help may be offered if necessary.

Many Unitarian Universalists depart from Christian tradition in their beliefs about the events that make up the Easter story, such as the bodily resurrection of Jesus. The word "resurrection" means coming back to life after death. Most Christians believe that Jesus was resurrected and that he came back to life after he died. Most Unitarian Universalists believe that Jesus died and his body did not come back to life. Even so, all of us can find deep meaning in the idea that those we love live on in our memories and that renewal or rebirth is available to us during our lifetime.

The date for the annual celebration of Easter is tied to both the historical event of the stories of Jesus' death and resurrection, according to Christian theology, and to factors associated with the spring equinox and spring festivals. In Western Christianity, Easter is on the first Sunday after the first full moon after the vernal equinox. In Eastern Christianity, Easter is on the first Sunday after the first full moon after the vernal equinox or after the end of Passover, whichever is later.

The biblical references for the crucifixion and resurrection of Jesus are: Matthew 27-28, Mark 15-16, Luke 23-24, John 18-20, and I Corinthians 15.

Session Plan

Gathering   Varies

As the children arrive greet each of them individually and hand them some Easter stickers to decorate the Christian Calendar and the *Special Times* sign on the poster. Hang the poster on the classroom door. Ask if they know which upcoming (or just passed) holy day is celebrated in Spring with flowers and the symbol of the cross.

Focusing   5 minutes

Gather the children in a circle on a rug or in chairs. Show them the basket of Easter symbols. Then ask, "What does your family do on Easter Sunday?" Bring in to the conversation any of the Christian Easter symbols that are not mentioned.

Conversation and Story   15 minutes

Say, "Today we're talking about Easter, which is always celebrated in the spring, in March or April. Can you tell me anything about how this special time began?" After allowing time for possible responses, ask, "Is Easter a Jewish or Christian holy day?" Say, or confirm, that it is a Christian holy day because it tells the story of how Jesus died.

Tell the story, "The Origins of Easter," or read from one of the suggested books if you prefer. Be cautious, however, about using words they may not understand or giving them more of the story than they need to know at this age. Too many details will confuse them.

Read the story, "The Origins of Easter."

After telling the story, ask the children what they heard and wait for their comments or questions. If someone should ask, "Did he really come back to life?" you might say, "As far as we know, once people, or animals, are dead, they are never able to come back to life. But some people think that even though our bodies die, there is a part of us that lives on. No one knows for sure. But we do know that people live on in the memories of those who knew them. We remember and talk about someone we loved who died. We remember what the person looked like, we can 'see' him or her in our minds. We can remember that person for our whole life!"

Engage the children in a conversation around this idea to help them become aware of the interwoven concepts of life, death, and immortality. Some ideas you might incorporate could include how long ago Jesus died. Tell the children that he died about 2,000 years ago, and people today still talk about him and celebrate his life, because those who knew him loved him and believed in what he taught. These people told others—their children and grandchildren who told their children and grandchildren. So, while a person who dies cannot come back to life, some of what she or he said and did will live on because people remember.

Also, include in your conversation ways in which people view death. Say, "Flowers are a sign of Easter, too. (Point to or hold up the lilies or other flowers you brought.) Lilies like this one are used in Easter celebrations because their pure white color reminds people of new hope and new beginnings. And when this flower dies, its seed can be planted again and a new flower will come up. In the fall, we plant bulbs which look almost dead, dry and brown, but lo and behold, in the spring up pops a tulip or daffodil! The flowers rise again. So Easter reminds us that living things always die but new babies are born, new flowers come up. Life begins and ends and begins again."

Song   5 minutes

When you sense that the children's attention is waning, invite them to sing, "Alleluia Sing." Stand and sing it through a couple of times.

Activity   20 minutes

Invite children to the craft table and tell them that you're going to make baskets of Easter symbols. Give each child a small basket and a copy of Resource 26. As the children make and arrange the different symbols in their basket, talk about the meaning of each one. Help the children place first the tissue paper inside their basket, then fill it with sand and cover the sand with Easter grass. Have the children color, cut out, and glue the Alleluia sunrise and the Hosanna palm to popsicle sticks. Help the children make a cross from two popsicle sticks. Then have them arrange their symbols along with fresh flowers in their baskets to take home.

Easter Snack   Varies

Enjoy your special snack together.

Closing Circle   5 minutes

Gather in a circle and invite each child to put his or her basket into the center. Light the chalice candle and say, "This Easter morning, we give thanks for the life of Jesus, for the new life of Spring, and for the new life we will have as we grow and change throughout our lives. Alleluia and Amen."

Evaluation and Planning

Were the children confused or disturbed by the story of Jesus' crucifixion and resurrection? Did they seem to understand the idea of the interweaving of life, death, and immortality? Do you think you need to follow up with the conversation in coming sessions?

What session comes next? Who will be responsible for which activities?

The Origins of Easter

On Palm Sunday, we told the story of how people greeted Jesus and his friends as they came into the city of Jerusalem—waving palm branches and shouting their welcome to him. Jesus was so popular with the people that the leaders of the city, particularly the priests, were afraid that the people would try to put Jesus in charge and make him king of the Jews. The priests tried to prove that Jesus was breaking the laws, so that they could arrest him.

The celebration of Passover began on Thursday night. After Jesus and his friends ate their Passover meal, they went to pray in the Garden of Gethsemane. After awhile, the priests' guards came, arrested him, and took him away.

On Friday morning, the priests turned Jesus over to the Roman governor, Pilate, saying that Jesus was trying to be named king of the Jews. The priests knew the Roman rulers would not like this, for they had appointed the king. Pilate knew the priests were jealous of Jesus, so he offered to let him go. But the crowd of people, whom the priests had incited against Jesus, was shouting for Jesus to be crucified. To crucify him meant to hang him on a cross until he died. Pilate had Jesus whipped and then handed him over to the soldiers to be crucified.

The soldiers put a crown of thorns on Jesus' head, made fun of him, gave him his cross, and sent him up a hill to be crucified. The crowd circled around him. By nine o'clock in the morning they had put him on the cross and by three o'clock in the afternoon he died.

A friend took Jesus' body and placed it in a tomb which was a little cave and a heavy stone was rolled across the entrance. On the third day after he died, two women came to the tomb and were surprised to find his body was gone.

Some of Jesus' friends said Jesus came to them after he died—that they saw and talked with him. Others said this couldn't be so.

Alleluia Sing!

Words & Music: Shelley Jackson Denham

Al - le - lu - ia, sing, sing a song of laugh - ter,
sing a song of joy, sing a song of love.
Sing a song of praise, sing a song of won - der,
Sing al - le - lu - ia, sing!
Al - le - lu - ia, Al - le - lu - ia,
Al - le - lu - - - ia!
Al - le - lu - ia, Al - - le - lu - ia,
Al - le - lu - ia, Al - le - lu - ia!

Session 21: A Time for Rebirth

22 A Time to Return Home— Yom ha-Atzmaut

Goals for Participants

- To learn of the joy of the Jewish people in founding the modern state of Israel.
- To reflect on the responsibilities of the dream of a homeland.

Materials

- Copies of Resource 27, "Star of David Pattern," for each participant
- Map of Middle East and Israel
- Cardboard or oaktag
- Scissors
- Tape or stapler
- String
- Cassette tape of the song, "Anu Banu Artza"
- Cassette player
- Pencils and markers
- Glitter
- Glue
- Chalice, candles, and matches
- Books on Israel for the Reading Corner

Preparation

- Make a sign "*Special Times* celebrates *Yom ha-Atzmaut* today" for the Unitarian Universalist poster.

- Recruit a dance/movement teacher to teach the Hora dance. Practice the dance steps yourself.

- Obtain a tape of the song "Anu Banu Artza," a traditional folktune to which the Hora is danced.

- Prepare to tell or read the stories, "The Simple Old Man" and "The Mother of Israel."

- Obtain all necessary materials and resources for activities and Special Corners.

Background

Since 1948, the return of the Jewish people to their homeland has been celebrated on the 5th of Iyyar (May 14), the date of the founding of the modern state of Israel. In Israel there are parties, performances, and parades. Yom ha-Atzmaut is preceded by Yom ha-Zikkarar, a day of remembering those who suffered and died for Israel. But the mood changes from sorrow to celebration on Yom ha-Atzmaut. Services in the synagogue include reading from the Book of Psalms and from the prophets. This verse from Isaiah 2:4 is often highlighted:

And they shall beat their swords into plowshares, and their spears into pruning hooks;
Nation shall not lift up sword against nation, neither shall they learn war any more.

Jews around the world focus their celebrations around the relationship between humanity, land, and the earth. The religious perspective of Yom ha-Atzmaut is becoming more and more a vision of universal Judaism rather than the particular birthday of the nation of Israel. It is a reflection of the balance of Diaspora (Jewish communities outside of Palestine or modern Israel) and Israel as two contemporary centers. It is also a deepening of the Jewish tradition connecting the future to the past.

For this session, you will need a modern map of Israel, but it would be helpful to look at a Bible atlas to see the ancient lands of the Middle East, too. Also in this session, there are stories of two individuals important in building the modern state of Israel. It would also be helpful to familiarize yourself briefly with other important leaders—Theodore Herzl, David Ben Gurion, and Golda Meir. *A Kid's Catalog of Israel,* by Chaya Burstein is an excellent children's resource book on this subject.

There is a great deal of "telling" in both the Focusing and Story activities. Keep the children's interest by breaking it up with different leaders taking different parts, or with music, or even act some of it out.

Session Plan

Gathering   Varies

Greet children as they arrive and hand out stickers to decorate the Jewish Calendar and the *Special Times* sign for the poster. Hang the poster on the classroom door. Engage them in a conversation about the Star of David by asking something like, "Where have you seen the Star of David?" Some responses would be on the Israeli flag, in decorations for synagogues, on Torah scrolls, and as an identifying symbol of the Jewish religion.

Before the Focusing activity, teach the Hora dance and tell the children that you will dance it a couple times in this session. The Hora has become the Jewish national dance. It has four basic steps that are repeated over and over. Dancers form a circle and hold hands or put hands on each other's shoulders. They dance to the right with grapevine steps or hops.

The following illustration shows a dancer with a white leg and a shaded leg. The dancer's *weight* is on the *shaded* leg. Once you've taught the steps, play "Anu Banu Artza" and start dancing.

Focusing   10 minutes

When everyone has arrived, move to the circle area. After everyone is settled, show them the map of Israel and the Middle East. Ask the children to name as many places on the map as they can, such as Jerusalem, Bethlehem, the Mediterranean Sea, the Dead Sea, the West Bank, the Jordan River, the Gaza Strip, Judah, and Mount Sinai.

Tie their answers into a commentary on Israel by saying something like, "Israel is a land of diverse cultures. It has been called the crossroads of the Middle East because it is a land bridge between Africa (to the west) and Europe and Asia (to the north and east).

"Over the centuries, it has been ruled by many different peoples and nations. In ancient times the area now known as Israel was inhabited by nomadic tribes. This was the Promised Land that Moses led his people into from the bonds of slavery in Egypt. About 3,000 years ago the kingdom of Israel split into the north and south regions. The name "Jew" comes from the name of that southern region, called Judah. David became their most wise and famous ruler and built their great temple.

"About 200 years after the kingdom of Israel split in two, conquerors came from the north and

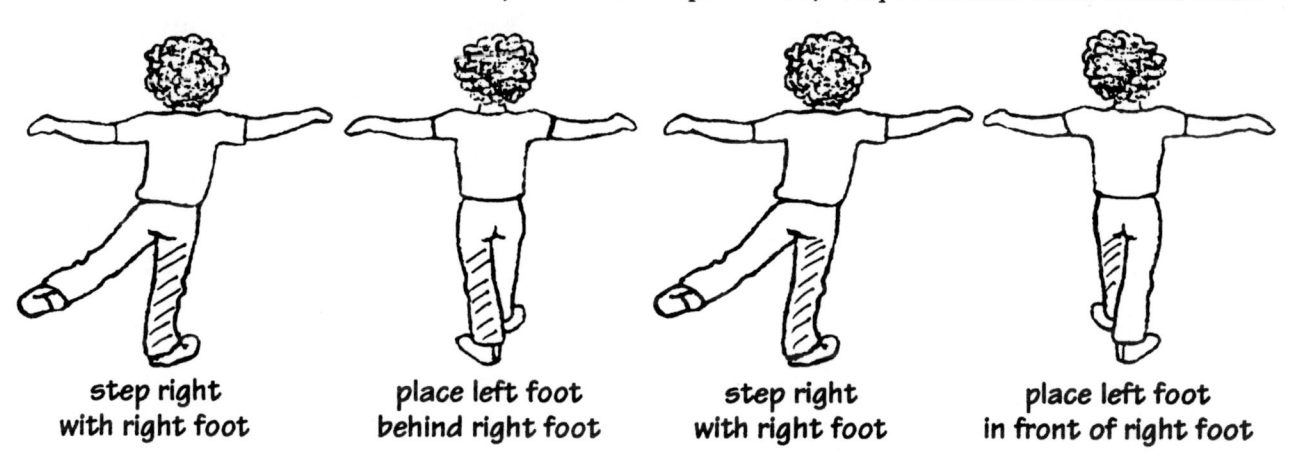

**step right
with right foot**

**place left foot
behind right foot**

**step right
with right foot**

**place left foot
in front of right foot**

Session 22: A Time to Return Home

then the Romans came. The Jews were taken away and over the centuries scattered to all parts of the world. They were exiled in strange lands in Europe, in Africa, in Asia, and later in America. Sometimes they were accepted in these foreign countries, but often they were forced to live in separate sections of town and pay high taxes. But wherever they lived, they always kept their hope and dream of returning to their land. Every year at the end of the Passover Seder they sang, 'To the next year in Jerusalem.'

"At the beginning of the twentieth century when the Jews in Europe were having an extremely difficult time, a new movement was born. It was called Zionism. Theodore Herzl was the leader of the movement and he believed that the Jewish people should live in a land of their own. He called a meeting of Jewish leaders from all over the world in 1897. He told them that in fifty years there could be a Jewish state and challenged them, 'If you will it—it is not a dream.'

"This morning we will learn about two people who helped bring that dream into reality. For indeed, 50 years after this first Zionist meeting, the new state of Israel was established in 1947."

Conversation and Story   20 minutes

Read the stories, "The Simple Old Man" and "The Mother of Israel."

After the first story, you may want to take a break and dance the Hora again with the children.

After the second story, engage the children in a conversation around some of the following questions:

- What did you hear in these stories?
- What if Aaron David Gordon said he was too old to inspire young people to become farmers in Israel?
- What if Henrietta Szold decided she could do nothing to help the children left with no parents in Europe?
- What if you dreamed your biggest dream to help others, what would that be?

Conclude the conversation with, "The United Nations voted to establish a national homeland for the Jews in 1947. On May 14, 1948, David Ben Gurion, the first Prime Minister of Israel, read the Declaration of Independence. The Jewish people everywhere went wild and danced and sang for joy. It was their first Yom ha-Aztmaut, Israel Independence Day. After 2,000 years, the Jews had a homeland."

Activities   20 minutes

Tell the children that they will be making hanging Stars of David. Pass out copies of Resource 27 to each child and have them trace the two Stars of David on cardboard and cut them out. Cut a slit in each star as shown.

Then fit the stars together and staple or tape the string to the point of the star. The children can decorate the stars with glitter or marker designs. If desired and appropriate, hang the stars up around the room.

If you've already taught the Hora, dance it again here.

Choices Time   Varies

The children can choose to browse among the books in the Reading Corner, to continue making Stars of David, or to continue dancing the Hora. Enjoy a snack if it is your custom.

Closing Circle   5 minutes

Light the chalice candle and say something like, "For the joy of having a place we call home, let us wish that everyone has a home. For the years of struggle and war, let us strive to live in peace with all people. Shalom."

Evaluation and Planning

What worked well?
　　What session will be used next week? What do we need to do to prepare?

The Simple, Old Man: Aaron David Gordon (1856-1922)

Aaron David Gordon sang as he chopped up the soil with his *touriya* (a short hoe) and laughed at his aching muscles. All his life Gordon had worked at a desk in a dusty Russian office, and finally, at age forty-eight, he threw away his stiff collar and dark suit and came to Palestine to be a farmer.

"The old man," his young fellow workers in Palestine called him. They said it with respect because the "old man" was the strongest of them all. When they couldn't get work from the farm owners and had barely enough money to buy bread and eggplant for supper, Gordon would pull them up to dance a Hora (circle dance) even though their stomachs were empty. "Herva," he would laugh, "we have the soil and our independence. What more do we need? Let's dance!"

Working and dancing were not enough for Gordon. He had to shout his joy at building a homeland to the whole Jewish world. He would wake up before dawn, tiptoe into the hall with his kerosene lamp so as not to wake the others, and write down his thoughts about a new way of life, a new religion for the Jewish people. It would be a religion of labor that would pull the Jews out of the crowded cities of Europe and bring them back to nature, to become farmers and workers in Palestine.

Life grew harder and more dangerous for Gordon and his comrades when World War I broke out. The Turks, who ruled Palestine, believed that the Jews were helping their enemies, the British. One day Turkish soldiers raided the area around Deganiah where Gordon lived. They locked all the men into a shed and dragged them out, one by one, to beat and torture them. The frightened settlers huddled together, hearing the sounds of blows and screams from the next room. Suddenly gaunt, white-bearded Aaron stood up and began to snap his fingers, sway, and sing this Yiddish song:

Let my enemies torment me,
Let them drain me drop by drop,
There's a happy song inside me
That no pain will ever stop.

During those hard years many Jewish settlers died, and others left Palestine. But Gordon kept writing, urging Jews outside Palestine to come and work the land.

After a day in the fields he would sit outside his little house in Kibbutz Deganiah, and neighbors would visit and talk with him about their hopes and worries. The children of Deganiah came to hear stories and sing with the "old man." A five year old explained that she like to come because "Grandpa Gordon is just like us, except he has a beard."

The Mother of Israel: Henrietta Szold (1860-1945)

Henrietta was the oldest of five daughters, and she wanted so much to be a boy. "Nonsense," said her father, a Baltimore rabbi. "You're as good as a son. Maybe better." They studied together, and she helped him with his writing and research. Together they started a school to teach English to Russian-Jewish immigrants. Later Henrietta helped to found the Jewish Publication Society and led a women's Zionist group called Hadassah. She studied at an all-male school—the Jewish Theological Seminary. Henrietta was the first woman ever to attend. But she had to promise that since she was a woman, she would not expect to graduate as a rabbi.

There it was. Being a woman in the late 1800s always seemed to stop her from doing big, important things. She knew that women had important work to do like homemaking and raising children. But as the years went by, she remained unmarried. By 1921, when Henrietta was sixty, she felt as though her life was nearly over and she hadn't done a thing with it! She couldn't imagine that her happiest and busiest time was just about to start.

Henrietta's organization, Hadassah, had set up health clinics in Palestine before the First World War. After the war Hadasssah built more clinics as well as hospitals, laboratories, and a nursing school. Henrietta came to Palestine to visit and stayed to direct the work. Only a few years later she took on a much harder task, one that would mean life or death to thousands of children.

Hitler had come to power in Germany and began to threaten and arrest German Jews. Reha Freir, a German-Jewish leader, persuaded parents to let their children travel to Palestine, where they would be safe. She crisscrossed Germany and nearby countries like a Pied Piper, pleading with worried parents and gathering boys and girls for the trip. It became Henrietta's job to take care of the children when they reached Palestine. She met them at the ship and found housing, youth leaders, and schools for them in kibbutzim and children's villages. She coaxed money from Hadassah and other organizations to pay the children's expenses. And she argued and bargained with the British to allow the children into Palestine. Each year more and more desperate parents sent their children to Henrietta. If only the British had allowed more entry certificates, thousands more children would have been saved.

On her seventy-fifth birthday Henrietta Szold was too busy to stop and rest, even for a day. "I have a great, new work ahead of me," she said. "I must get young people out of Germany, and after that out of France, Lithuania, and Russia. What does age mean? Nothing!"

This huge rescue operation was called Youth Aliya. It saved 170,000 European boys and girls in the 1930s and 1940s. Many of them never saw their parents again. The gentle lady with soft, brown eyes and white hair who met the children at the dock became a second mother to them.

23 A Time to Do Right—Shavuot

Goals for Participants

- To learn the origins of Shavuot, the Jewish celebration of the Giving of the Law.
- To explore and articulate "Rules for Living."

Materials

- Stickers of stone tablets, Torah scroll, books, sheaves of wheat, and fruits or flowers
- Torah scroll used in Session 6 (Simhat Torah) and/or a representation of stone tablets. Often Bible storybooks have illustrations of the tablets.
- Pictures, scrolls, and flags of Simhat Torah from Session 6 if they still exist.
- Wheat, barley, dates, grapes, figs, pomegranates, olives, and flowers (optional, see Background)
- Large sheets of newsprint
- Pencils and markers
- Self-drying clay
- Wax paper
- Rolling pins (child size), one for every three children
- Plastic knives
- Wooden skewers or clay tools
- Cheese blintzes or cheesecake
- Milk
- Paper cups and napkins
- Chalice, candles, and matches
- Books for the Reading Corner, such as:
    All About Jewish Holidays and Customs, by Morris Epstein
    Jewish Days and Holidays, by Greer Fay Cashman
    Jewish Holiday Fun, by Judith Hoffman Corwin
    My Very Own Shavuot Book, by Judyth Saypol and Madeline Wikler
    Picture Book of Jewish Holidays, by David A. Adler
    Poems for Jewish Holidays, by Myra C. Livingston

Preparation

- Read through the entire session plan and decide who will lead each activity.

- Make a sign "*Special Times* celebrates *Shavuot* today" for the Unitarian Universalist poster.

- If you have a copy machine that enlarges, make a Ten Commandment poster out of Resource 28 by photocopying it at the highest enlargement, or print the commandments on a large sheet of newsprint, and post it on a wall.

- Make cardboard patterns of two stone tablets for each child to trace and create their own clay tablets. Or use a stencil from a Jewish stencil book if you have one.

- Recruit sufficient adult or youth assistance to help with the clay tablet activity.

- Obtain all necessary materials for the activities and Special Corners.

Background

Shavuot is a holiday of nature and a holiday of history. Shavuot, the Jewish "Feast of Weeks"—so called because it falls seven weeks after Passover—celebrates the return of Moses to his people from the top of Mount Sinai in the desert, bringing with him two stone tablets with God's Ten Commandments on them. These laws are the basis of the Torah and the Jewish faith.

Shavuot celebrates also the harvesting of wheat and the ripening of the first fruits. The celebration recalls the bringing of some of those fruits to the Temple in Jerusalem long ago. Shavuot is often observed by feasting on a dairy meal which symbolizes the promised land, the land of "milk and honey." Flowers and greenery are placed around homes and synagogues on this occasion.

Shavuot reminds the Jewish people that God and human beings are partners. They believe God created the earth, sun, and rain and that people plant seeds and work in the fields. Together a more fruitful world is created. They believe God gave Jews the Torah and they follow its laws and teachings. Together a better world is created.

Shavuot celebrates the giving of the Torah which spelled out the details of the Covenant between God and the Jewish people. For the religious Jew, Sinai is the experiencing of the Divine—faith in a God who cares about this world and expects his people to lead good and just lives. On Shavuot Jews go to the synagogue and read from the Book of Ruth, which tells of her conversion to Judaism.

This celebration concludes the cycle of Jewish holidays which began with Rosh Hashanah.

Session Plan

Gathering   Varies

As the children arrive greet them individually and hand out the stickers to decorate the Jewish Calendar and the *Special Times* sign for the poster. Hang the poster on the classroom door. Say, "This morning we'll be learning about the Jewish festival of Shavuot. This is the last Jewish holiday in our *Special Times* year. Maybe you remember that the first one we learned about was Rosh Hashanah, last September." Invite them to browse among the books in the Reading Corner, especially the books on Jewish holidays.

Focusing   5 minutes

Gather in a circle in chairs or on a rug. Show the objects you have brought—Torah scrolls, stone tablets, or the food items associated with Shavuot. Ask if they remember what the Torah is—the book or books of Jewish Laws and stories that the Jewish people read in their temple services. Then say, "The special time we celebrate today is called Shavuot. It is another Jewish holiday that celebrates the Torah, especially the Laws."

Conversation and Story   20 minutes

Ask the children where laws come from and who makes them. Their responses might include their parents and police. They may say the president or the prime minister! Then ask, "Do you think there are some things that people would just *know* are the right thing to do, so we should not have to have laws about them? What would some of those things be?" You could mention worth and dignity of each person, freedom to grow and be yourself, compassion for others, etc.

Show the children pictures, scrolls, and flags from the Simhat Torah session if you still have them, and ask if they remember that celebration. You will probably need to say a few things about it to prod their memories—October was a long time ago!

After recalling that holiday, say, "Shavuot, which we celebrate today, comes seven weeks after Pesah or Passover. In fact, *shavuot* means the Feast of Weeks. It celebrates the time when God gave Moses the Ten Commandments (the Law) and told him to take them to his people, the Hebrews. This is what happened.

"As you may remember from the story of Passover, the Jewish people had been slaves in Egypt, and then Moses led them out of Egypt across the Red Sea. After they escaped from the pharaoh's soldiers, the people wandered in the desert. Moses told them that he was taking them to the Promised Land, the 'land of milk and honey.' It was a very hard trip, and they were hungry and discouraged by the time they camped at the foot of Mount Sinai. Mountains were considered holy places then.

"One day, there was thunder and lightning

and a thick cloud covered the mountain. God had come down to the mountaintop in fire and smoke, and the mountain shook violently. God called Moses to come to the top of the mountain, saying, 'Come up to me on the mountain and wait there; I will give you the tablets of stone, with the law and the commandments, which I have written for the people.' So Moses climbed to the top of the mountain and brought down two stone tablets with the Laws. We call those Laws the Ten Commandments."

Put the poster on the wall at their eye level and read each commandment out loud.

Ask, "Have you ever heard of these ten commandments?" It's possible that none have, although some may. Explain the meaning of each briefly and simply.

Then say, "Shavuot celebrates the time when God gave the Ten Commandments to the people. Many Jewish people decorate their homes with beautiful flowers at this time because it also has become a celebration of the spring harvest. Let's make a poster with our own ideas about what kind of rules (laws) we should have for how we live."

Activities   10 minutes

Post a sheet of newsprint on the wall at eye level and gather around it. Ask the children for their ideas of good rules for living. Say, "What rules would be good for everyone to follow? For example, if I said everyone should wear a heavy jacket and boots when it's cold and snowing, that's not a rule for people who live where it never gets very cold and never snows, is it?"

Print and/or sketch on newsprint the rules they suggest. Then ask them which of these rules they think everyone should live by while they are together here on Sunday mornings. Place a check next to those. Display the sheet of rules on a bulletin board or wall for the remaining sessions.

For the next 15 minutes, engage the children in making clay tablets. Assign an adult or teenage assistant to every three or four children and give each of them a cardboard pattern for the tablets.

Give each child a sheet of wax paper and place on it a small ball of clay (about 1 1/2" in diameter). Give each child another piece of wax paper to put over the ball of clay, and a plastic knife. Tell them to take turns with the rolling pins and to roll out the clay very thin.

The assistant will trace the pattern of two tablets onto the rolled out clay with a skewer or clay tool. Tell the children to use the plastic knife to cut away the excess clay from around the outline, and to print *one* commandment on each tablet. The assistants can help them to simplify the wording to two or three words, such as "Love God," "Don't Kill," "Don't Lie," and so on, and help those children who have difficulty doing this.

Choices Time   Varies

As the children complete their work on the project or grow restless, invite them to look at books in the Reading Corner or to work at the Gardening Window. Ask for volunteers to help you put out the blintzes or cheesecake, cups of milk, and napkins for the closing circle.

Closing Circle   5 minutes

Gather in a circle around the table and share a snack of cheese blintzes or cheesecake and milk in honor of "the land of milk and honey."

Light the chalice candle and close by saying, "We are thankful for countries where people live by just laws. We pray that someday all people will live by just laws in their countries. Let us work to make the laws we live by even better. Shalom."

Evaluation and Planning

What went well? What might have worked better?

This concludes the Jewish holidays for the year. What planning ahead do we need to do for the remaining sessions? Are there materials that must be ordered and if so, who will do that?

24 A Time for Wondering about God—Always

Goals for Participants

- To explore concepts of God.
- To discover that there are many ways to think about God.
- To experience with others a time for wondering about God.

Materials

- A shell, stone, flower, and other natural object(s) or pictures of mountains, ocean waves, a newborn baby, etc.
- Stickers of any natural object (see above)
- Large sheet of slick paper for fingerpainting
- Fingerpaints in a good selection of colors (or sufficient containers of primary colors so that the children may combine them as they like)
- Smocks
- Cassette tape recording of a variety of nature sounds
- Cassette player
- Seeds or small plants to put in the Gardening Window or outdoors
- Chalice, candle, and matches
- Books for the Reading Corner, such as:
  What is God?, by Etan Boritzer
  Old Turtle, by Douglas Wood
  Conversations With Children, by Edith F. Hunter
  The Creation, translated and adapted by Stephen Mitchell
  Children's Letters To God, by Stuart Hample, et al.
  Dear God: Children's Letters, by David Heller
  When Do You Talk to God?, by Patricia and Frederick McKissack

Preparation

- Think through your own concepts about God.
- Read through the entire session plan and decide who will lead each activity.
- Make a sign "*Special Times* celebrates *God* today" for the Unitarian Universalist poster.
- Look at the Conversation and Story activity and plan how you will conduct the discussion about God.
- Decide which book to read, *What is God?*, by Etan Boritzer, or *Old Turtle*, by Douglas Wood. Obtain a copy to use for this session.
- Plan for a quick cleanup after the fingerpainting activity.
- Obtain all necessary materials for activities and Special Corners.

Background

Unitarian Universalists hold widely differing concepts of God. Each person's ideas are valid. Our hope is that leaders will be open to divergent views of God and encourage another's views, especially the children's. Wonder comes so naturally to young children. It is always appropriate to say something like, "People have lots of different thoughts about . . . ," or "No one really knows for sure, but some people say . . . "And, of course, your own honest response to a child's question, "What do you believe?" is always appropriate. It is our responsibility as adults, parents, and teachers to be sensitive to each child's evolving sense of the divine or holy. There is much we can learn from children as we nurture their spiritual growth.

Many of us find it easier to think and wonder about the universe, how it came to be, and what is meant by its existence, than to talk, think, and wonder about a deity. Surely there is much in the universe for each of us to wonder about! It is often through these wonderings that thoughts of God emerge.

The story for this session is either *What Is God?*, by Etan Boritzer or *Old Turtle,* by Douglas Wood. Choose which story you will read or tell and become familiar with it.

Session Plan

Gathering   Varies

Play the tape of nature sounds softly as you greet the children individually. Hand out stickers to decorate the *Special Times* sign for the poster. Hang the poster on the classroom door. Engage the children in conversation about whatever the stickers depict, a flower, mountain, tree, etc.

Focusing   5 minutes

Gather in a circle, on chairs or on a rug. Sit quietly and look at the object or objects you have chosen: an intricate shell, a smooth stone, a flower, etc. Say, "Whenever I see (name object), I always find myself wondering about so many things. Today our special time is a time for wondering about God."

Conversation and Story   30 minutes

Ask, "How do you answer the question, 'What is God?'" Encourage the children to express their own ideas of who and what God is to them. Then ask, "What makes you think that?" Listen carefully to each answer.

Then say something like, "There are lots of different ideas about God, aren't there? Let's listen to a story about wonderings and then talk some more about God."

Read the story, *Old Turtle* or *What Is God?*

In the book, *What Is God?* by Etan Boritzer, find excerpts to stimulate the children's discussion of God. The ideas presented in it can be the basis of many discussions about God. Choose a few and let the children take off from them, one at a time.

Or you might begin with, "God is something or someone that people everywhere have wondered about. You mentioned several things when I asked you what God is when we were talking before I read the story. You said God is (mention the ideas the children gave). And I've heard people say God is (mention a few concepts the children may not have said, such as a force, the Creator who made the world, our father, our mother, a Goddess, love, a spirit, like a mountain).

"These are all things that God is. What have you heard that God *does*?" Encourage their responses. If they don't mention it you could add, "I've heard people say, 'God made the world,' 'God makes something where there was nothing,' 'God makes things grow,' 'God can do anything,' and so on.

"Some say there is one god. That's what Jewish and Christian people believe, and it's what some Unitarian Universalists believe. There are others who believe there are many gods. Who is right? Oh, so many things to wonder about!

"Can we see God? Touch God? Feel God? Can we *know* there is a god? Will people someday know?" Allow time for responses.

Then ask, "Is it all right *not* to believe in god?"

Bring the discussion to a close with the poem, "Who Has Seen the Wind?" Say, "Here is a poem some people like to read when they are wondering about God."

> Who has seen the wind?
>   Neither I nor you.
> But when the leaves hang trembling,
>   The wind is passing through.
> Who has seen the wind?
>   Neither you nor I.
> But when the trees bow down their heads,
>   The wind is passing by.
>   —Christina G. Rossetti

Say, "We can't see the wind, but we know it's there. We can't see God, and we wonder if God really is. And so we go on wondering, wondering, and wondering."

Activity   15 minutes

Encourage the children to keep wondering as they fingerpaint and listen to music. Spread sheets of paper on tables or on the floor and give the children smocks to put on. When they have chosen their colors and have begun painting, start playing the tape of nature sounds and tell them to paint what they are feeling. End the painting when it is time to cleanup and get ready for the Closing Circle.

Choices Time   Varies

When the children complete or tire of fingerpainting and are cleaned up, point out the choices available: the Reading Corner, seeds or seedlings to plant, and any other choices you have provided.

Closing Circle   5 minutes

Gather in a circle and light the chalice candle. Say, "May we never stop wondering about important things—life, death, love, how things grow, the universe, and God. So be it!"

Evaluation and Planning

What worked well? What might have been better planned?

Were insights gained from this session that might be used on future Sunday mornings? Should we continue discussions about God?

What session will follow? If your next session is Everybody's Birthday, Session 25, remember to mail a letter (see Resources 29) to each participant.

25 A Time When Each Person is Special—Everybody's Birthday

Goals for Participants

- To explore the concept that all people are important.
- To participate in a celebration where all are honored.

Materials

- Copies of Resource 29, "Birthday Letter to Parents," for each participant.
- Stickers of birthday cakes or party hats
- A copy of the book, *On the Day You Were Born,* by Debra Frazier
- Books and/or additional photos of babies
- Large sheet of light-colored construction paper or posterboard
- Markers, crayons, pencils, and pens
- Large sheets of gold or yellow construction paper
- Long rope
- Roll of foil
- Yarn or ribbon
- Safety pins
- Scissors
- Glue and tape
- Unfrosted cupcakes
- Prepared cake frosting
- Plastic knives
- Birthday candles
- Instant camera and film
- Chalice, candle, and matches
- Picture books about babies and the following books for the Reading Corner:
  Everybody Has a Birthday, by Caroline Arnold
  Why Was I Adopted? by Carole Livingston
  Happy Birthday, by Gail Gibbons

Preparation

- Read through the entire session plan and decide who will lead each activity.

- Early in the week, make copies of Resource 29 and mail them to each participant before this session meets.

- Make a sign "*Special Times* celebrates *Everybody's Birthday* today" for the Unitarian Universalist poster.

- Prepare to tell or read "On the Day You Were Born."

- Make enough copies of Resource 30, "Star Pattern," so you have stars for each participant. Cut out the stars and set them aside for the children to create medals.

- Recruit a photographer, or take pictures of the children yourself.

- Bring in baby pictures of yourself.

- Make a large sign that says, "Unitarian Universalists believe that all people are important, no matter how young or how old," and hang it on the wall.

- Create a large birthday card by printing every child's name on a large sheet of construction paper or posterboard. Leave it on a table for children to write on.

- Create a Birthday rope by tying the ends of a long rope to make a circle.

- Obtain all necessary materials for activities and Special Corners.

Background

This session is designed to be a festive special time with songs, stories, games, and refreshments. These expressive activities give the children an opportunity to experience the joy of celebrating their own specialness *and* the satisfaction of honoring each other's uniqueness. *New Games* books have many cooperative games you may want to add to this session.

You may want to invite the children's parents to the last part of this session and make it an intergenerational celebration, but check with the children and decide. Choose a plan that will work the best with your group. Enjoy!

Session Plan

Gathering   Varies

As the children arrive, greet them individually, and hand out stickers to decorate the *Special Times* sign for the poster. Hang the poster on the classroom door. Find their names and birthdates on the Birthday Calendar and invite them to put stickers around their names on the calendar. Talk with them about their baby pictures. Collect the pictures, making sure their names are on the back or that you know which picture belongs to which child. If any children arrive without pictures, ask them to look at the baby books in the Reading Corner and find a picture that looks like them as a baby.

Focusing   10 minutes

Gather in a circle on chairs or on a rug. Hold up the pictures and ask the children to guess whose picture it is. For children who arrived without pictures, ask "Did you find a picture that looked like you as a baby?"

Conversation and Story   15 minutes

Say, "Today we're celebrating the birthdays of some very important, special people—you! Unitarian Universalists think that each person and all people are important. Let me read to you a story about birthdays."

Read the story, *On the Day Your Were Born.*

Afterwards, say, "Birthdays are a good time for thinking about all we have accomplished since our first birthday (the day we were born) and all of the things we want to be able to do in the future.

"What can you do now that you couldn't do on your birthday last year (or this time last year)? Can you remember what you could do when you were four?" After responses, say, "Even though today probably isn't your real birthday, you can still make birthday wishes. And when we celebrate everyone's birthday together, we shall all make birthday wishes! Does anyone have any wishes you would like to tell us?" Allow time for responses and discussion.

Say, "Now, let's write some birthday wishes for one another."

Activities   20 minutes

Tell the children to walk around the table where you left the large sheet with their names. Ask them to write a birthday wish for each other on the giant birthday card.

After the children have signed the card, invite them to make medals for themselves.

Have the children select a sheet of construction paper and a star pattern. Ask them to trace the pattern and cut it out. Punch a hole in the star to thread yarn or ribbon. Print *Special* or *Special Person* and their name. Insert the yarn or ribbon through the hole and tie it. Pin the medal to their shirts, or attach it to their clothing with masking tape.

After the children have made their medals, say "Let's play some birthday games!" Play the Circle Game from Session 1, *Adras*, Israeli Tic-Tac-Toe from Session 6, the Birthday Tug of Joy, and other cooperative games appropriate for young children.

To play Birthday Tug of Joy, put the Birthday rope on the floor. Ask everyone to sit in a circle on the floor outside the Birthday rope. Tell the children the Birthday Tug of Joy is when everyone in the circle rises to a standing position at the same time by pulling on the rope. Ask each person to hold the rope with both hands and pull herself or himself up. Count to three and say "up!" Keep trying until all are standing. Then invite the children to give themselves a joyful cheer.

Then invite each person to spread frosting on a cupcake and choose a birthday candle to place on top of it. While some children are frosting their cupcakes, have the others pose for their photographs while wearing their medals.

Closing Circle   10 minutes

Light the birthday candles and sing "Happy Birthday." You may wish to change the words to something like:

Happy Birthday to me,
Happy Birthday to you,
Happy Birthday everyone,
Happy Birthday to us.

Blow out the candles and eat the cupcakes!

Light the chalice candle and say something like, "We believe every person is important, no matter how young, no matter how old. On this day, when we celebrate everybody's birthday, know that you are special. Go forth into the world as the special person you are!"

Be sure baby pictures and the pictures taken today are taken home.

Evaluation and Planning

What worked well? Did the children enjoy games and story?

If your next class is the final session, Closing Sunday, review the session thoroughly and remember to mail a letter (see Resource 31) to each participant.

26 A Time to Say "Good-bye"— Closing Sunday

Goals for Participants

- To integrate what they learned this year.
- To celebrate the year of *Special Times*.

Materials

- Copies of Resource 33, "Star of David, Cross, and Flaming Chalice Symbols," for each participant
- Calendars, crafts, snapshots, and other items from the year's activities
- Stickers from all sessions
- Songs you choose to sing
- T-shirts (synthetic or part synthetic)
- Fabric crayons
- White paper
- Refreshments for Closing Circle
- Chalice, candle, and matches
- Books for the Reading Corner, especially your favorites from the year, including: *I'm in Charge of Celebrations,* by Byrd Baylor

Preparation

- Read through the entire session plan and decide who will lead each activity.

- Early in the week, make copies of Resource 31 for each participant and mail them before the session meets.

- Make a sign "*Special Times* celebrates *Closing Sunday* today" for the Unitarian Universalist poster.

- Choose some songs from the year's collection to sing. Recruit a song leader if necessary.

- Recruit additional help for the T-shirt project.

- Bring extra T-shirts in case some children forget theirs.

- Make a poster out of the *Special Times* Game Board by enlarging it on the photocopier, or redrawing it on posterboard.

- Collect all items made during the year that should go home with the children today.

- Collect or make copies of all stickers and symbols used throughout the year.

- Obtain all necessary materials for activities and Special Corners.

- Bring in refreshments of your choice for Closing Circle.

Background

Throughout today's activities, reflect on the year's program and remember the special times you have shared. Help the children look forward to the next step in their religious education journey. Will they move into multi-age summer activities? Will they have a summer break and be in a new group in the fall? Try to make connections that will help them see continuity in their religious education program and their connection to the whole UU congregation.

Tailor this final session to fit the plans of your group and your congregation. You may want to elaborate on the final celebration; you may want to involve parents and families in the Closing Circle. Make it a festive occasion, yet add a feeling of closure for the end of the program.

118 Special Times

Session Plan

Gathering — 5 minutes

As the children gather, look around and talk about the four calendars, the craft items, and the snapshots. Ask, "What was your favorite special time this year?" Decorate the *Special Times* sign for the poster. Hang the poster on the classroom door. Look through your collection of *Special Times* signs from the past 25 sessions.

Focusing — 10 minutes

Ask the children to gather in a circle. When everyone is settled, say, "We have celebrated many special times this year. The stickers on our calendars and on our *Special Times* signs will remind you of them." Give the children a few minutes to look at all the stickers.

Ask, "What kinds of holidays did we celebrate this year? Can you remember which were Jewish? Christian? What other special times did we observe? (Thanksgiving, Birthday, etc.)"

Special Times Game — 15 minutes

Invite the children to play a game by saying, "Let's play a *Special Times* Game. Let's first play a guessing game. I'll name a story or a person and you tell me which special time it belongs with and if it is a Christian or Jewish holiday." Place the *Special Times* Game Board poster at their eye level. Ask some of the following questions:

- When did Simcha shout "Hosanna!"?
- When is the story of Jonah and the Whale told?
- When did we hear about the Inuit who brought song and dance to his people?
- When did we hear about Esther and Mordechai and Haman?
- Do you remember which Sunday we talked about Samuel May, Elizabeth Blackwell, Whitney Young, and Amos Peck Seaman?
- When did we hear about The Three Wise Men or The Three Kings?
- When did we talk about Moses and the Ten Commandments?
- The story of Mary, Joseph, and a baby are told at what time of the year?
- When did we talk about the Unitarian Universalist Service Committee and welcoming "guests at our tables?"
- When did each of us blow out a candle on a cupcake?

Then pass out at least ten stickers to each child. Go around the circle and have each child match one sticker symbol to a special time square on the game board. Continue around the circle matching symbols to special times until all the sticker symbols are on the game board. The goal is to identify and match quickly, cooperative help is to be encouraged.

Activity — 15 minutes

Explain the following to the children:

"To make a *Special Times* T-shirt, we'll sketch our designs on a sheet of paper. Choose some of your favorite celebrations, or use the symbols on the handout I just gave you. Then draw those pictures on the shirt with a fabric crayon. You can draw one large picture of something, or draw lots of small ones to represent several of those special times. If you'd like, print 'SPECIAL TIMES' and your name on your T-shirt, or have everyone autograph your T-shirt."

Tell them to press down with the fabric crayon to make the lettering dark.

The children may wish to put on their shirts and wear them for the remainder of the session.

Singing — 5-10 minutes

Then say, "Let's sing some of our favorite songs from the year." With everyone joining in, sing the songs to instrumental accompaniment if possible.

Some songs that are especially appropriate are "We've Got the Whole World In Our Hands," which can be found at the end of this session, "Make New Friends," or "Love is a Circle."

Closing Circle — 5 minutes

Light the chalice candle and ask each child and

leader to complete this sentence: "One special time I will remember is _____."

Then say, "We have had special times together all year, and this is the special time when we must say good-bye for a while. May we keep one another in our hearts. Shalom."

Close with an appropriate song, such as "Shalom."

Have refreshments and then help the children collect items to take home.

Evaluation and Planning

Be sure to return materials and supplies to the location(s) requested. What suggestions would you make for the future use of this *Special Times* material?

We've Got the Whole World in Our Hands

Words: Jan Evans-Tiller

Music: Traditional

1. We've got the whole world in our hands. We've got the whole wide world in our hands. We've got the whole world in our hands. We've got the whole world in our hands.

2. We've got the trees and flowers in our hands.
3. We've got the birds and the fishes in our hands.
4. We've got the lakes and the forests in our hands.
5. We've got the towns and the cities in our hands.

Encourage the children to contribute suggestions for other stanzas. End each stanza with "We've got the whole world in our hands."

Bibliography

Many of these books and resources are available from the UUA Bookstore, 25 Beacon Street, Boston, MA 02108.

Children's Books Used in This Program

Boritzer, Etan. *What is God?* Willowdale, Ontario: Firefly Books, Ltd., 1990. (Session 24)

Frazier, Debra. *On the Day You Were Born.* San Diego, CA: Harcourt Brace Jovanovich, Inc., 1991. (Session 25)

Giono, Jean. *The Man Who Planted Trees.* Post Mills, VT: Chelsea Green Publishing Co., 1987. (Session 15)

Mellonie, Byron and Robert Ingpen. *Lifetimes: The Beautiful Way to Explain Death to Children.* Toronto/New York: Bantam Doubleday Dell, 1987. (Session 9)

Mitchell, Steven. *The Creation.* New York: Dial Press, 1990. (Session 2)

White Deer of Autumn. *The Great Change.* Hillsboro, OR: Beyond Words Publishing, Inc., 1992. (Session 9)

Wood, Douglas. *Old Turtle.* Duluth, MN: Pfeifer-Hamilton Publishers, 1991. (Session 24)

Books for Teachers and/or Religious Education Library

Allison, Linda. *The Reasons for Seasons: The Great Megagalactic Trip Without Moving From Your Chair.* Boston: Little Brown, 1975.

Cashman, Greer Fay. *Jewish Days and Holidays.* New York: SBS Publishing, Inc., USA Edition, 1979.

de Paola, Tomie. *Book of Bible Stories, New International Version.* New York: Holiday House, 1987.

____. *The Parables of Jesus.* New York: Holiday House, 1987.

Holmo, Joan. *Celebrating the Church With Young Children.* Collegeville, MN: The Liturgical Press, 1988.

May, Herbert. *Oxford Bible Atlas.* New York: Oxford University Press, 1985.

Parry, Caroline. *Let's Celebrate: Canada's Special Days.* Toronto: Kids Can Press Ltd., 1987.

Smith-Durland, Eugenia. *To Celebrate: Reshaping Holidays and Rites of Passage.* Ellenwood, GA: Alternatives, 1987.

Strassfeld, Michael. *The Jewish Holidays, A Guide and Commentary.* New York: Harper & Row, 1985.

van Straalen, Alice. *The Book of Holidays Around the World.* New York: Dutton, 1985.

Resources for Activities

Burstein, Chaya. *A Kid's Catalog of Israel.* New York: Jewish Publishing Society, 1988.

Fluegelman, Andrew, Editor. *The New Games Book.* New York: Doubleday, 1976.

____. *More New Games.* New York: Doubleday, 1981.

Maguire, Jack. *Creative Storytelling: Choosing, Inventing, and Sharing Tales for Children.* New York: McGraw Hill, 1985.

Roehlekepartain, Jolene. *Fidget Busters: 101 Quick Attention-Getters for Children's Ministry.* Loveland, CO: Group Publishing, Inc., 1992.

Supplementary Books for Reading Corner

Adler, David A. *A Picture Book of Jewish Holidays.* New York: Holiday House, 1981 and 1982.

___. *A Picture Book of Passover.* New York: Holiday House, 1982.

Alcott, Louisa May. *An Old-Fashioned Thanksgiving.* New York: Holiday House, 1989. (This story was first published in *St. Nicholas Magazine* in November 1881.)

Anderson, Joan. *The First Thanksgiving Feast.* New York: Tichnor & Fields, Clarion Books, 1984.

Arnold, Caroline. *Everybody Has a Birthday.* New York and Toronto: Franklin Watts, 1987.

___. *What We Do When Someone Dies.* New York: Franklin Watts, 1987.

Baylor, Byrd. *I'm in Charge of Celebrations.* New York: MacMillan, 1986.

Bolognese, Don. *A New Day.* New York: Delacorte Press, 1970.

Brotman, Charlene and Barbara Marshman. *Holidays and Holy Days.* Lexington, MA: Brotman-Marshman, 1983.

Brown, Margaret Wise. *Christmas in the Barn.* New York: Crowell, 1952.

___. *The Dead Bird.* New York: HarperCollins Publishers, Inc., 1989.

Chaikin, Miriam. *Sound of Shofar: The Meaning of Rosh Hoshanah and Yom Kippur.* New York: Tichnor & Fields, 1986.

Cohen, Miriam. *Will I Have a Friend?* New York: MacMillan, 1967.

Corwin, Judith Hoffman. *Jewish Holiday Fun.* Englewood Cliffs, NJ: Julian Messner, 1987.

De Gasztold, Carmen B. Rumer Godden, translator. *Prayers from the Ark.* New York: Penguin, 1992.

de Paolo, Tomie. *The Christmas Pageant: From the Text of Matthew and Luke.* Minneapolis, MN: Winston Press, 1978.

___. *Francis, the Poor Man of Assisi.* New York: Holiday House, 1982.

___. *Nana Upstairs, Nana Downstairs.* New York: Putnam, 1973.

___. *The Miracles of Jesus.* New York: Holiday House, 1987.

___. *The Story of the Three Wise Kings.* New York: Putnam, 1983.

Drucker, Malka. *Hannukah. Eight Nights, Eight Lights.* New York: Holiday House, 1980.

___. *Passover, A Season of Freedom.* New York: Holiday House, 1982.

Fassler, Joan. *My Grandpa Died Today.* New York: Human Science Press, 1983.

Fahs, Sophia Lyon. *From Long Ago and Many Lands.* Boston: Skinner House, 1988.

Fisher, Aileen. *Jeanne d'Arc.* New York: Crowell, 1970.

Gibbons, Gail. *Happy Birthday.* New York: Holiday House, 1986.

___. *Thanksgiving Day.* New York: Holiday House, 1983.

___. *Easter.* New York: Holiday House, 1989.

Gillis, Elizabeth. *People Like Us.* Boston: Society of the First and Second Church, 1989.

Gooding, Margaret K. *Exploring Our Roots.* Toronto: Canadian Unitarian Council, 1988.

Grollman, Earl A. *Explaining Death to Children.* Boston: Beacon Press, 1969.

Guthrie, Donna. *A Rose for Abby.* Nashville, TN: Abingdon Press, 1988.

Hample, Stuart, et al. *Children's Letters to God.* New York: Workman Publishers Co., Inc., 1991.

Hays, Wilma Pitchford. *Patrick of Ireland.* New York: Coward-McCann, 1970.

Heller, David. *Dear God: Children's Letters.* New York: Doubleday and Co., Inc., 1987.

Hoagland, Victor, C.P. *The Book of Saints, the Lives of Saints According to the Liturgical Calendar.* New York: Regina Press, 1986.

Hollerorth, Barbara. *The Haunting House.* Boston: Unitarian Universalist Association, 1974. (Out of print)

Hunter, Edith F. *Conversations With Children.* Boston: Unitarian Universalist Association, 1982.

Hutton, Warwick. *Jonah and the Great Fish.* New York: MacMillan, 1984.

Jupo, Frank. *The Thanksgiving Book.* New York: Dodd, Mead, 1980. (Includes harvest festivals from around the world.)

Kalman, Bobbie and Tina Holdcraft. *We Celebrate New Year.* Toronto: Crabtree Publishing Company, 1985.

Korelak, Jenny. *Hannukah. The Festival of Lights.* New York: Lorthrop, Lee & Shephard, 1990.

Krementz, Jill. *How It Feels When a Parent Dies.* New York: Alfred A. Knopf, Inc., 1988.

Bibliography 123

LaChapelle, Delores and Janet Bourque. *Earth Festivals*. Silverton, CO: Finn Hill Arts Publishers, 1974.

Lindgren, Astrid. *Christmas in the Stable*. New York: Coward McCann, 1962.

Livingston, Carole. *Why Was I Adopted?* New York: Lyle Stuart, 1978.

Livingston, Myra C. *Celebrations*. New York: Holiday House, 1985.

____. *Poems for Jewish Holidays*. New York: Holiday House, 1986.

Lobel, Arnold. *Frog and Toad Are Friends*. New York: Harper & Row, 1970.

McKissack, Patricia and Frederick. *When Do You Talk to God?* Minneapolis, MN: Augsburg, 1985.

Modell, Frank. *One Zillion Valentines*. New York: Greenwillow Books, 1983.

Munsch, Robert N. *Love You Forever*. Buffalo, NY: Firefly Books, 1986.

Post, W. Ellwood. *Saints, Signs, and Symbols*. Wilton, CT: Morehouse Publishing, 1974.

Prelutsky, Jack. *It's Valentine's Day*. New York: Greenwillow Books, 1983.

Roberts, Elizabeth and Elias Amidon, Editors. *Earth Prayers from Around the World*. San Francisco: Harper, 1991.

Sanford, Doris. *It Must Hurt a Lot: A Child's Book About Death*. Portland, OR: Multnomah Press, 1985.

Savary, Louis, M., S.T.D. *The Children's Book of Saints*. New York: Regina Press, 1986.

Saypol, Judyth and Madeline Wikler. *My Very Own Haggadah*. Rockville, MD: Kar-Ben Copies, Inc., 1983.

____. *My Very Own Megillah*. Rockville, MD: Kar-Ben Copies, Inc., 1977.

____. *My Very Own Shavuot Book*. Rockville, MD: Kar-Ben Copies, Inc., 1982.

Schwarts, Lynne Sharon. *The Four Questions*. New York: Dial Books, 1989.

Scheninger, Ann. *Valentine Friends*. New York: Viking Kestrel, 1988. (Published simultaneously in Canada by Viking Penguin.)

Silverman, Maida. *Festival of Freedom: The Story of Passover*. New York: Simon & Schuster, 1988.

Slate, Joseph. *Who Is Coming to Our House?* New York: Putnam, 1988.

Spier, Peter. *Book of Jonah*. New York: Doubleday and Co., Inc., 1985.

____. *Noah's Ark*. New York: Dell Publishing Co., Inc., 1992.

Staines, Bill. *All God's Critters Got a Place in the Choir*. New York: Dutton Children's Books, 1989.

Tracy, Denise. *A Stream of Living Souls*. Oak Park, IL: Delphi Resources, 1987.

Tudor, Tasha. *A Time to Keep: The Tash Tudor Book of Holidays*. New York: Rand McNally, 1977.

Viorst, Judith. *The Tenth Good Thing About Barney*. New York: Athenaeum, 1975.

Waber, Bernard. *Ira Says Goodbye*. Boston: Houghton Mifflin, 1988.

Westerhoff, John H., III. *Pilgrim People: Learning Through the Church Year*. San Francisco: Harper & Row, 1984.

Wilkin, Esther. *The Golden Treasury of Prayers for Boys and Girls*. New York: Golden Press, 1976.

Winthrop, Elizabeth. *A Child is Born: The Christmas Story*. New York: Holiday House, 1983.

Yolen, Jane. *Ring of Earth: A Child's Book of Seasons*. New York: Harcourt Brace Jovanovich, Inc., 1986.

Zolotow, Charlotte. *My Grandson Lew*. New York: Harper & Row, 1974.

Organizations

For excellent Jewish children's books:
KAR-BEN COPIES, INC.
6800 Tildenwood Lane
Rockville, MD 20852
301-984-8733

For information and resources about cooperative games:
New Games Foundation
P.O. Box 7901
San Francisco, CA 94120

Index to Resources

Resource 1:	Jewish Calendar	126
Resource 2:	Christian Calendar	127
Resource 3:	Unitarian Universalist Calendar	128
Resource 4:	Birthday Calendar	129
Resource 5:	Rosh Hashanah Letter to Participants and Parents	130
Resource 6:	Rosh Hashanah Symbols	131
Resource 7:	Sukkot Letter to Participants	132
Resource 8:	Simhat Torah Flag	133
Resource 9:	St. Francis Day Letter to Participants	134
Resource 10:	All Souls' Day Letter to Participants and Parents	135
Resource 11:	Thanksgiving Letter to Participants and Parents	136
Resource 12:	Dreidel Pattern	137
Resource 13:	Advent Calendar Pattern	138
Resource 14:	Advent Pocket Decorations	139
Resource 15:	Advent List of Activities	140
Resource 16:	Advent Letter to Parents	141
Resource 17:	"Each Night A Child is Born is a Holy Night"	142
Resource 18:	*Special Times* Chalice Tablecloth	143
Resource 19:	Heart Patterns	144
Resource 20:	Purim Letter to Participants	145
Resource 21:	Patterns for Purim Crown and Haman's Hat	146
Resource 22:	Lenten Letter to Participants and Parents	147
Resource 23:	Flaming Chalice Symbol	148
Resource 24:	The Four Questions	149
Resource 25:	The Lord's Prayer	150
Resource 26:	Easter Symbols	151
Resource 27:	Star of David Pattern	152
Resource 28:	The Ten Commandments	153
Resource 29:	Birthday Letter to Parents	154
Resource 30:	Star Pattern	155
Resource 31:	*Special Times* Letter to Participants	156
Resource 32:	*Special Times* Game Board	157
Resource 33:	Star of David, Cross, and Flaming Chalice Symbols	158

Jewish Calendar

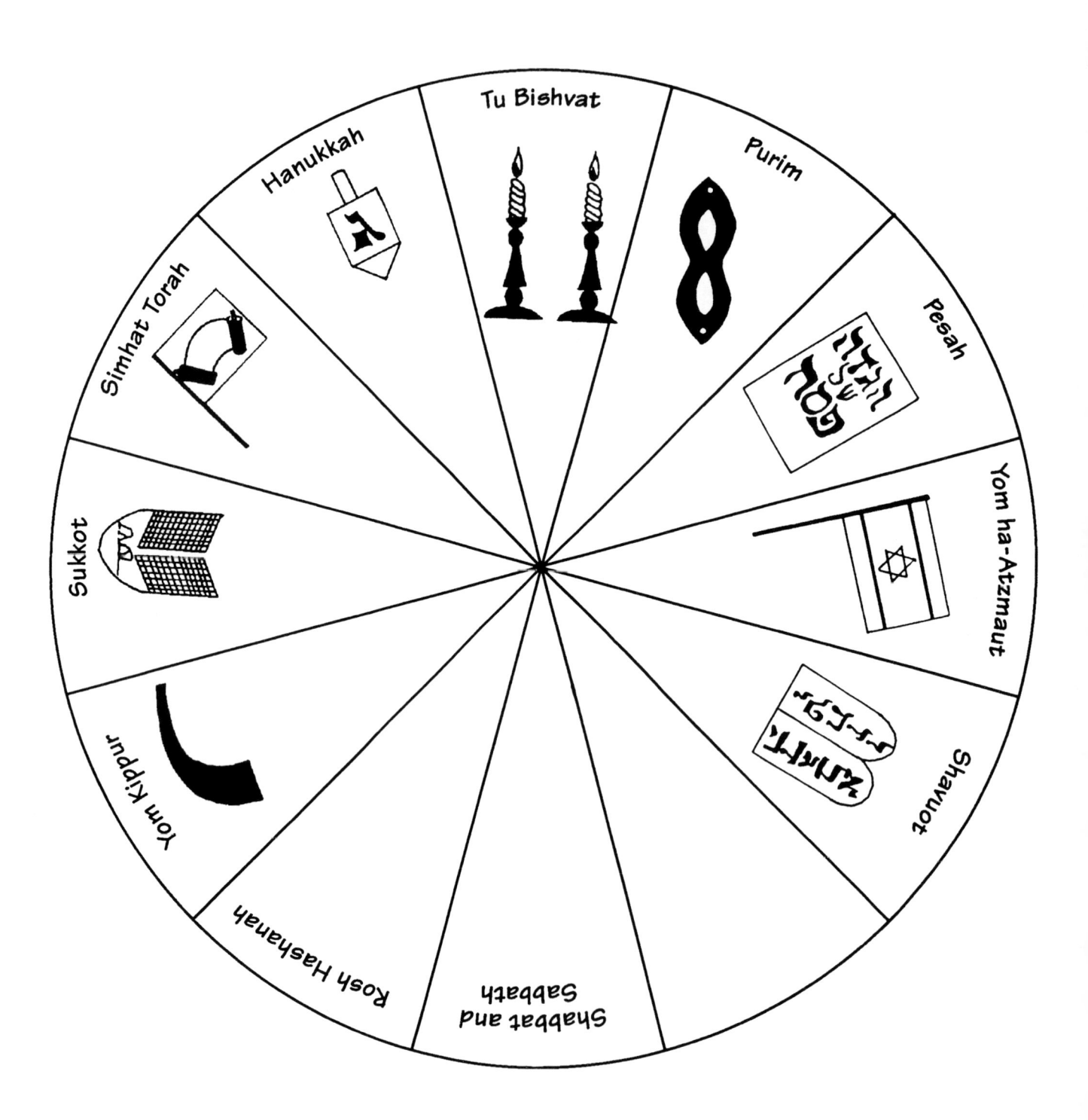

RESOURCE 1

Segments of the wheel (clockwise from top): Tu Bishvat, Purim, Pesah, Yom ha-Atzmaut, Shavuot, Shabbat and Sabbath, Rosh Hashanah, Yom Kippur, Sukkot, Simhat Torah, Hanukkah.

126 Special Times Unitarian Universalist Association

Christian Calendar

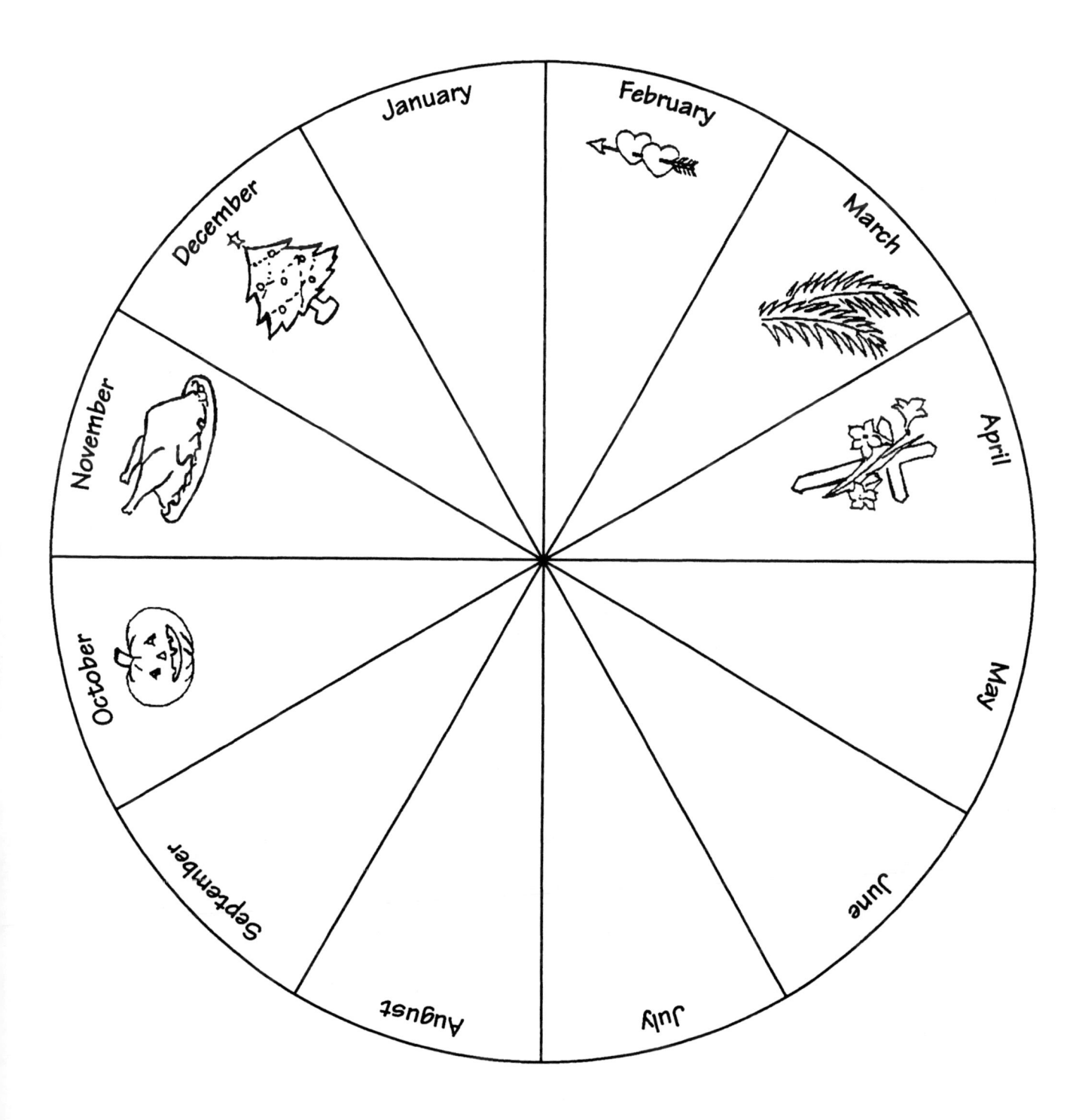

RESOURCE 2

Special Times — Unitarian Universalist Association — 127

RESOURCE 3

Unitarian Universalist Calendar

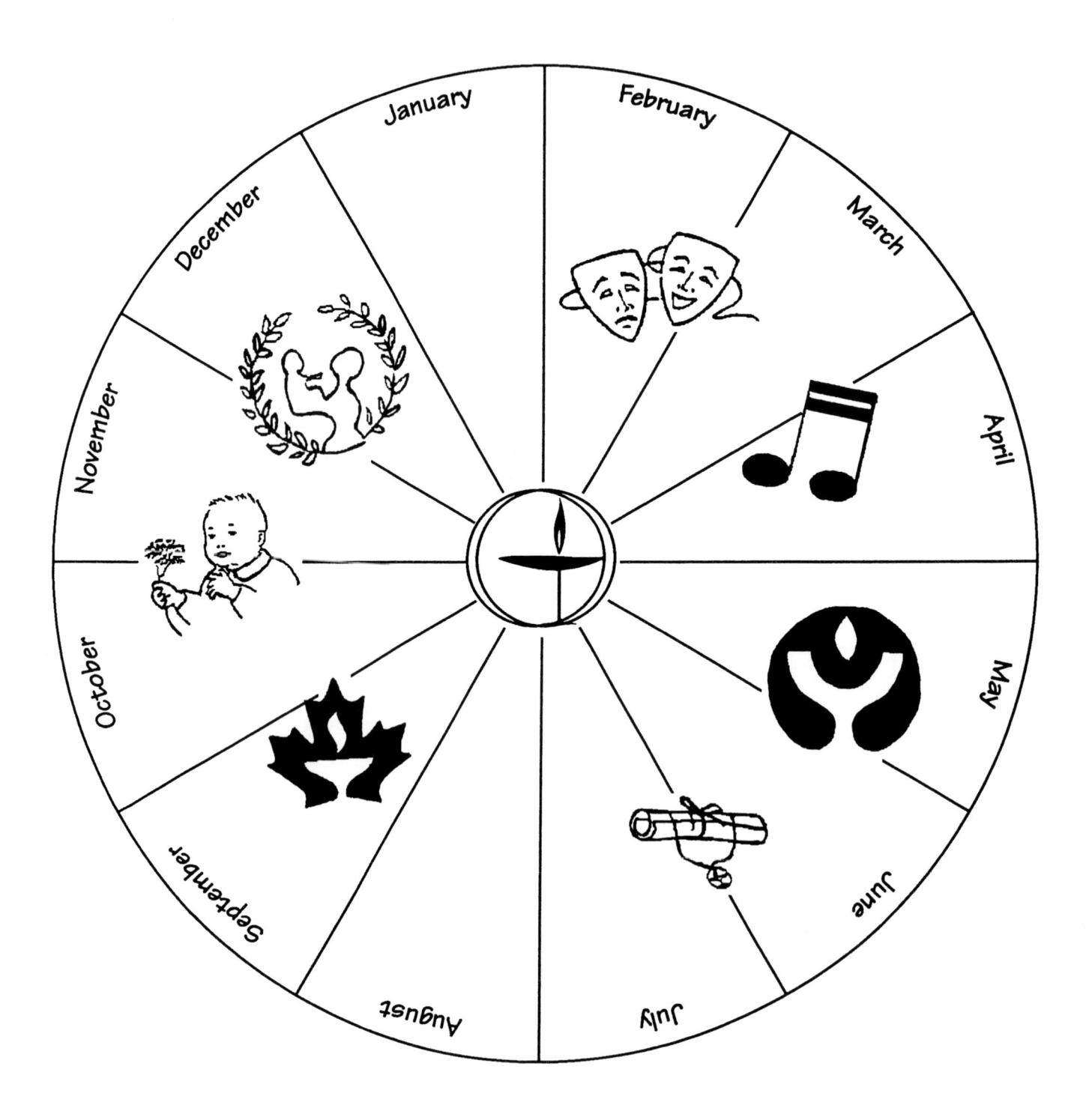

128   *Special Times*   Unitarian Universalist Association

Birthday Calendar

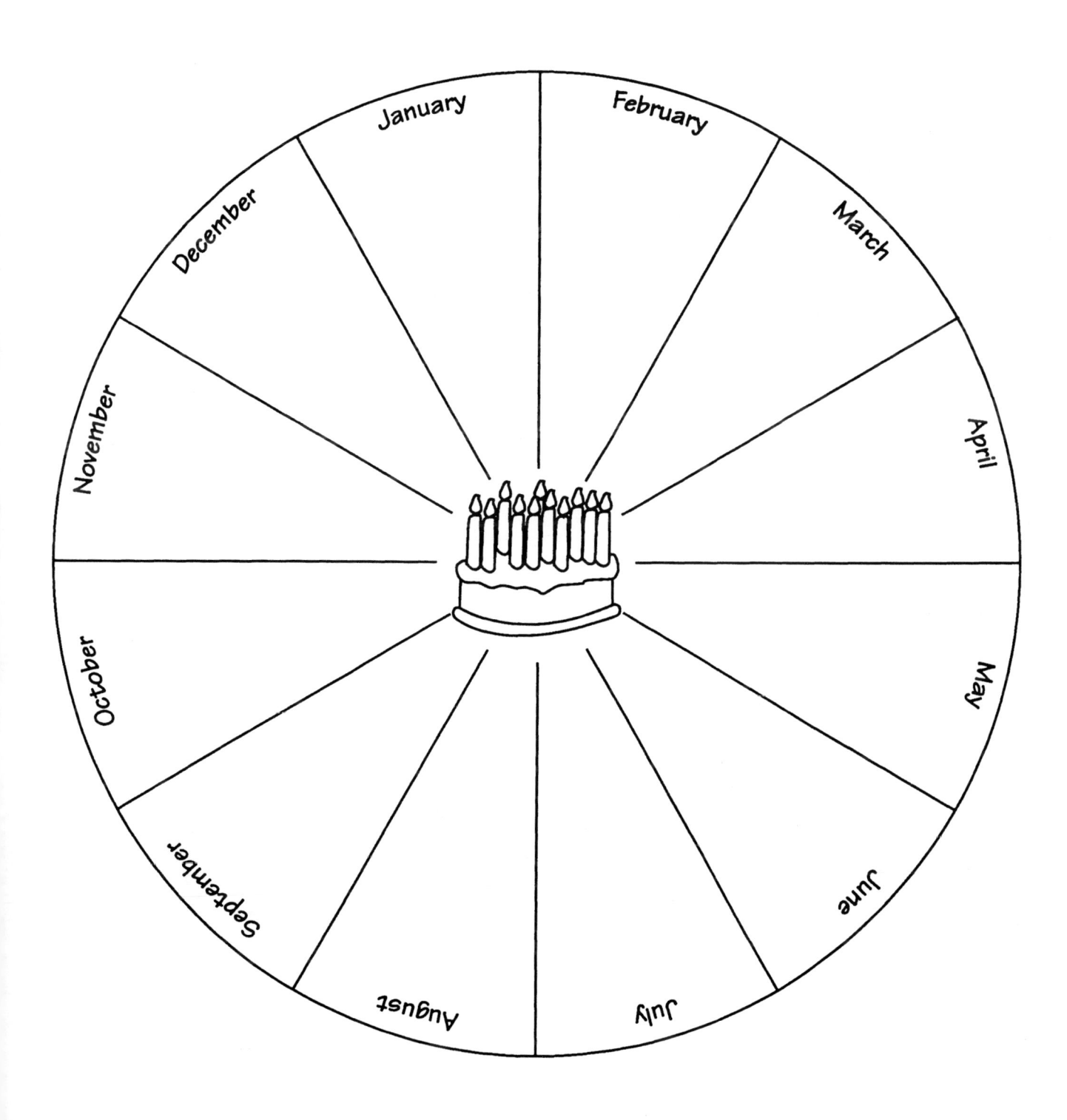

January
February
March
April
May
June
July
August
September
October
November
December

Special Times · Unitarian Universalist Association

Rosh Hashanah Letter to Participants and Parents

Note: If you want to use postcards instead of letters, reduce this letter accordingly, or rewrite it to fit the format you're using.

Dear

Hello! We have begun our *Special Times* program, celebrating the specialness of each person on our first Sunday. Last Sunday we learned about Shabbat, or the Sabbath, as an important time for worship for Jews, Christians, and Unitarian Universalists. We made a Creation mural which we would like to share with you.

This Sunday we will honor the Jewish special time, Rosh Hashanah. We will talk about changes, new beginnings, and a new year. The following Sunday we will talk about forgiveness and celebrate Yom Kippur.

We are happy your child, _____, is in our group and we look forward to welcoming you in our room on _____. Please come after worship service next Sunday to see our mural and to discuss with us future *Special Times* activities.

See you Sunday!

Sincerely,

Special Times Leaders

Rosh Hashanah Symbols

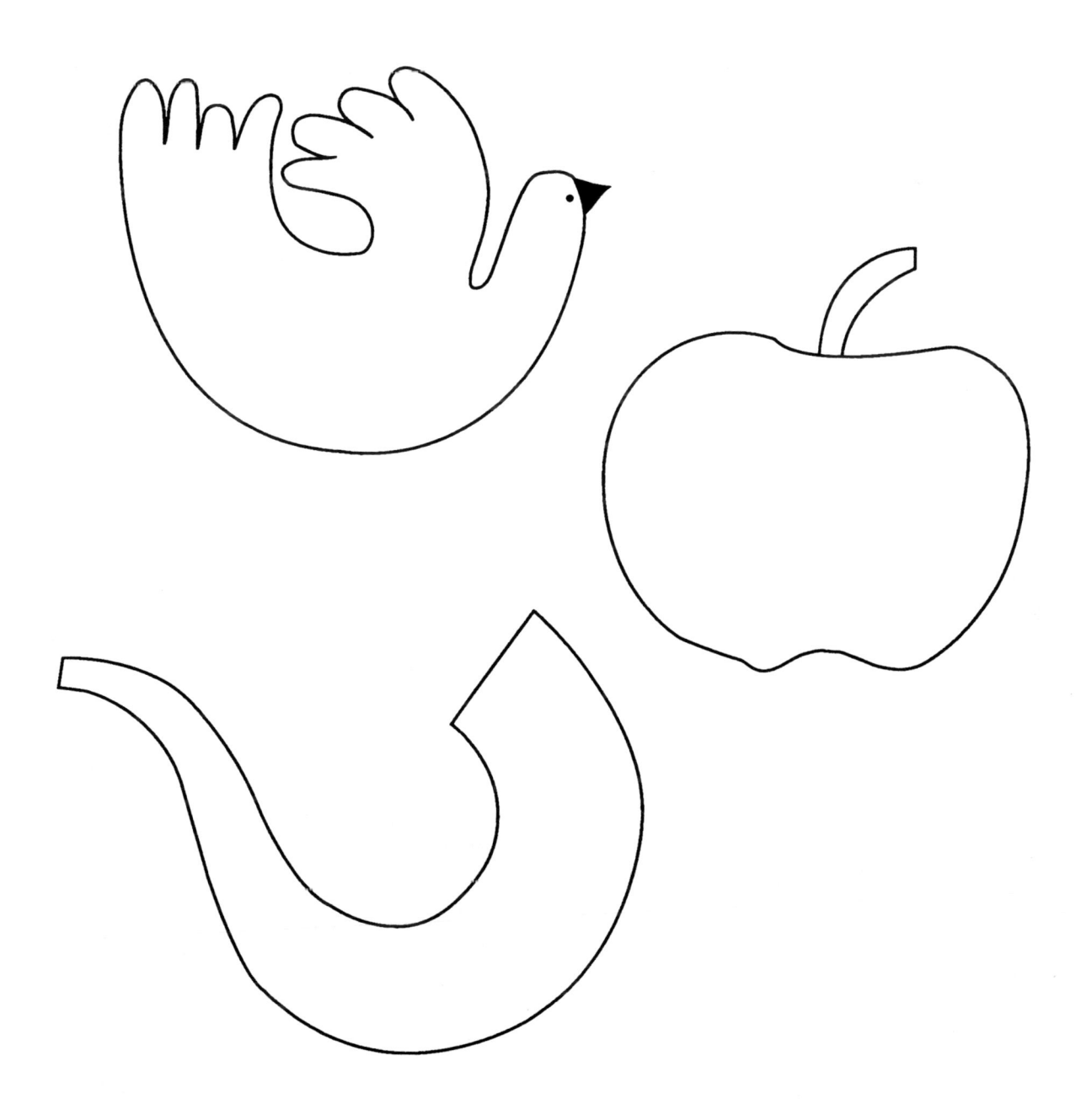

Special Times   Unitarian Universalist Association   131

Sukkot Letter to Participants

Note: If you want to use postcards instead of letters, reduce this letter accordingly, or rewrite it to fit the format you're using.

Dear

Next Sunday we will celebrate Sukkot, the Jewish harvest festival. We will have a sukkah—a booth like the Jews had long ago when they lived in the wilderness—and would like to decorate it with real fruits of the harvest. Will you bring a turnip, or potato, or some other fruit or vegetable recently harvested, that is, picked from the field or tree? If you want to bring more than one, that's fine. After our session, we will give the food to _____ where it will be appreciated and used to feed _____.

See you Sunday!

Special Times Leaders

Simhat Torah Flag

RESOURCE 8

design here

1. Make from white cardboard.
2. Color designs in the center from Simhat Torah flag symbols.
3. Decorate border designs.
4. Attach top or bottom side to dowel to make flag.

Special Times   Unitarian Universalist Association   133

St. Francis Day Letter to Participants

Note: If you want to use postcards instead of letters, reduce this letter accordingly, or rewrite it to fit the format you're using.

Dear

Next Sunday we will learn about St. Francis and have a ceremony of "Blessing the Animals." Do you have a pet? Please bring a picture of your pet or your favorite stuffed animal for our ceremony.

We will also bless other animals, such as those who are endangered species. If you like, bring a picture of one you are especially interested in for our discussions.

Please talk this over with your parents right away. We need some parent helpers, too! Please call one of us if your parents would like to help this Sunday.

Shalom,

Special Times Leaders

Telephone number:

All Souls' Day Letter to Parents and Participants

Note: If you want to use postcards instead of letters, reduce this letter accordingly, or rewrite it to fit the format you're using.

Dear

Hello! We have been enjoying special times from our Christian heritage these last couple of Sundays—All Saints' Day and St. Francis' Day. This Sunday we will be honoring the special time that is All Souls' Day by reading a beautiful book called _____.

Our group will be talking about All Souls' Day as a time to remember those who have died. We will talk about people who have died and light candles to their memory. Children will have an opportunity to work with clay, play dough, or finger paints to help deal with any feelings which may emerge.

We would appreciate it if your child could bring a picture of a person who has died. It could perhaps be a grandparent, even if your child did not know the person. We will take good care of the pictures and return them after our class. You are invited to visit our classroom after our session this Sunday, _____. If there is anything we should know about your child's experience with death, please call one of us before Sunday.

Shalom,

Special Times Leaders

Telephone number:

Thanksgiving Letter to Families of the *Special Times* Class

Note: If you want to use postcards instead of letters, reduce this letter accordingly, or rewrite it to fit the format you're using.

Dear

We invite you to visit our room at the end of our session on Sunday, _____, at _____, to share a time of thankfulness and to join us for a treat.

If you would like, bring an item of beauty for our celebration table.

We hope to see you then.

Shalom,

Special Times Leaders

Dreidel Pattern

Cut hole

turner: roll and insert in top of dreidel

Special Times   Unitarian Universalist Association   137

Advent Calendar Pattern

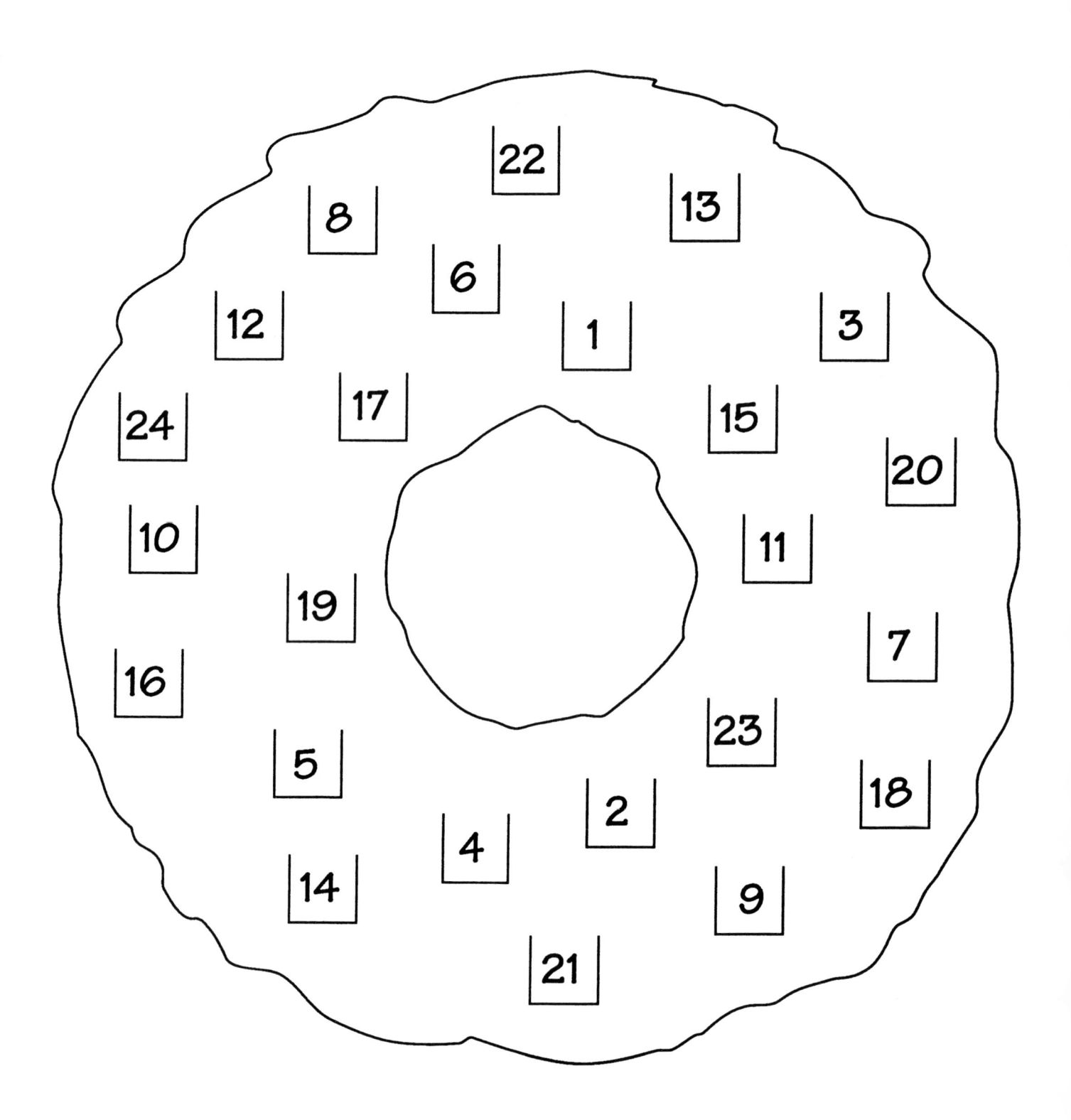

RESOURCE 13

138 *Special Times* Unitarian Universalist Association

Advent Pocket Decorations

Advent List of Activities

1. Give your mom or dad a hug and kiss and say, "Happy December!"
2. Pick out a favorite book and share it with someone.
3. Give a smile to someone older than you.
4. Remember to hang up your jacket today.
5. Make your own bed today.
6. Help make dinner tonight.
7. Do something nice for someone younger than you.
8. Give a special smile to your teacher.
9. Sing one of your favorite songs with your family at dinner. You choose the song!
10. Put a note under each person's pillow: "Dear _____, I like you because _____!"
11. Invite a friend to the library.
12. Try to fix something that is broken. You can ask for help!
13. How many things can you find that are red?
14. Make a holiday card for your teacher.
15. Draw a picture of your family and put it in a place where everyone can enjoy it.
16. Offer to set the table tonight and make a holiday centerpiece.
17. Ten days until Hannukah! Find out all you can about it.
18. Find out how to say "Hello" in two different languages! Teach them to someone.
19. Be on the look-out for litter. Pick it up and throw it in the trash!
20. Talk to your family about your favorite holiday customs. Ask about theirs.
21. How many things can you find that are green?
22. Make some Christmas cookies with your family.
23. Take a walk around the neighborhood with a family member. Greet everyone you see!
24. Ask your family to read aloud with you a favorite Christmas story.

Advent Letter to Parents

Note: If you want to use postcards instead of letters, reduce this letter accordingly, or rewrite it to fit the format you're using.

Dear Parents:

Seasons Greetings!

The children in our *Special Times* group made Advent calendars today. Your child may need to finish her or his wreath at home. Each of the 24 pockets on the wreath can be decorated on the outside (patterns enclosed in envelope). Inside each pocket is an activity for your child to do to prepare for and enjoy the Christmas season. In the spirit of cooperation and service, please help your child do each of the 24 activities.

We hope this Advent calendar will add meaning and joy to you and your family throughout the season.

Happy Holidays!

Peace,

Special Times Leaders

Each Night a Child is Born is a Holy Night

by Sophia Lyon Fahs

For so the children come
And so they have been coming.
Always in the same way they come—
Born of the seed of man and woman.
No angels herald their beginnings.
No prophets predict their future courses.
No wise men see a star to show
    where to find the babe that will save humankind.
Yet each night a child is born is a holy night.
Fathers and mothers—sitting beside their children's cribs—
Feel glory in the sight of a new life beginning.
They ask where and how will the new life end?
Or will it never end?
Each night a child is born is a holy night—
A time for singing.
A time for wondering,
A time for worshipping.

Special Times Chalice Table Cloth

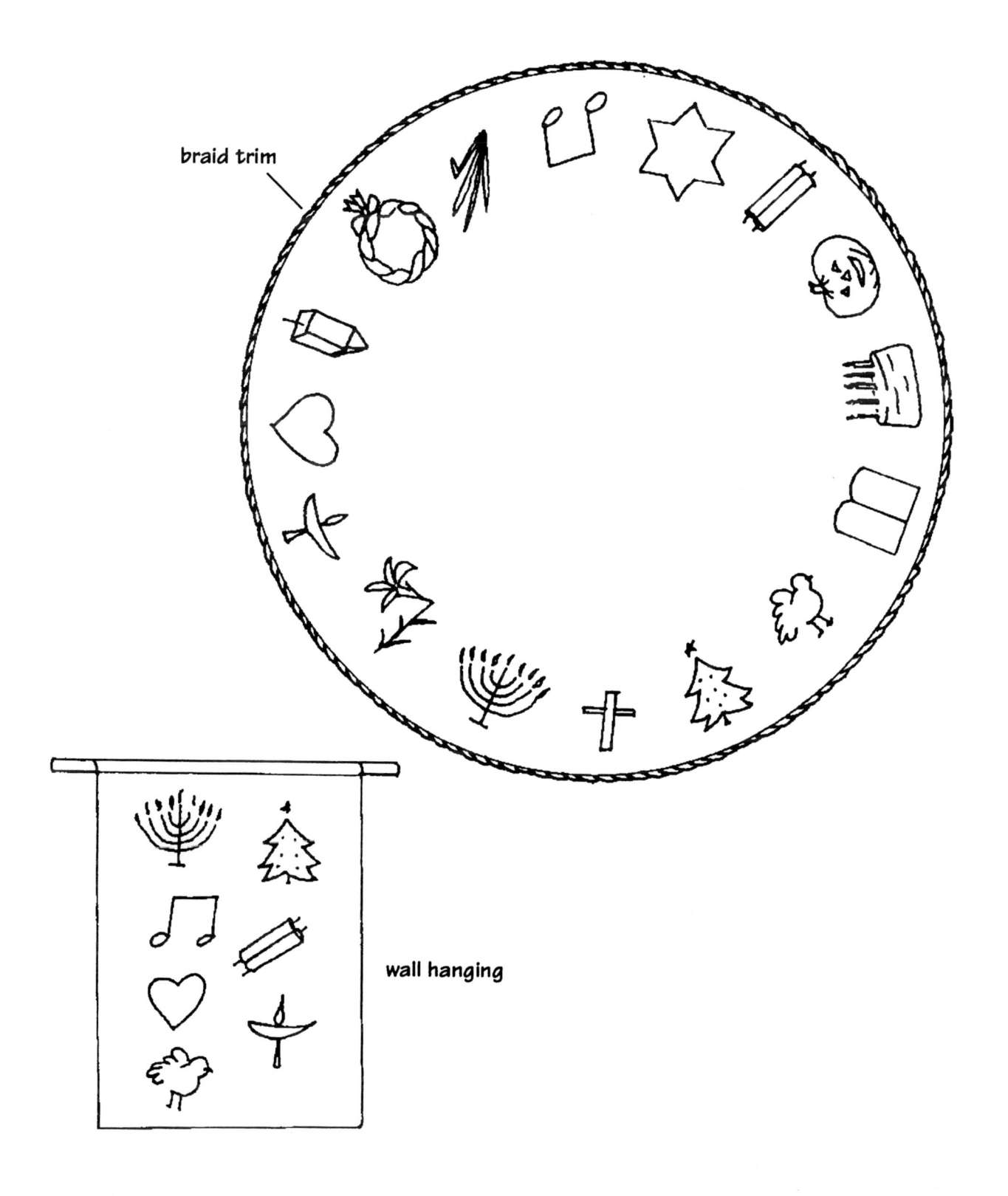

braid trim

wall hanging

Special Times   Unitarian Universalist Association

Heart Patterns

RESOURCE 19

144 *Special Times* Unitarian Universalist Association

Purim Letter to Participants

Note: If you want to use postcards instead of letters, reduce this letter accordingly, or rewrite it to fit the format you're using.

Dear

Next Sunday we will celebrate Purim, the happiest of Jewish holidays. It celebrates the story of Esther and Mordechai and how they saved the Jewish people. One Purim custom is to have a party. Please bring a traditional treat to share. Hamantaschen, the special Purim cookies, are sometimes available at bakeries. We are enclosing a recipe if you and an older person in your family would like to make some and bring them to class on Sunday.

Hamantaschen
1/4 lb. margarine
1/2 cup sugar
2 eggs, slightly beaten
2 cups flour
2 tsp. baking power
1 tsp. vanilla

Blend all ingredients. Roll out, cut into circles, and add your favorite filling. The traditional fillings are poppy seeds, apricots, or chopped prunes and raisins, but jelly or chocolate chips can be used, too. Fold the dough over the filling in 3 folds and pinch the corners. Bake at 350° for 25-30 minutes.

Shalom,

Special Times Leaders

Pattern for Purim Crown and Haman's Hat

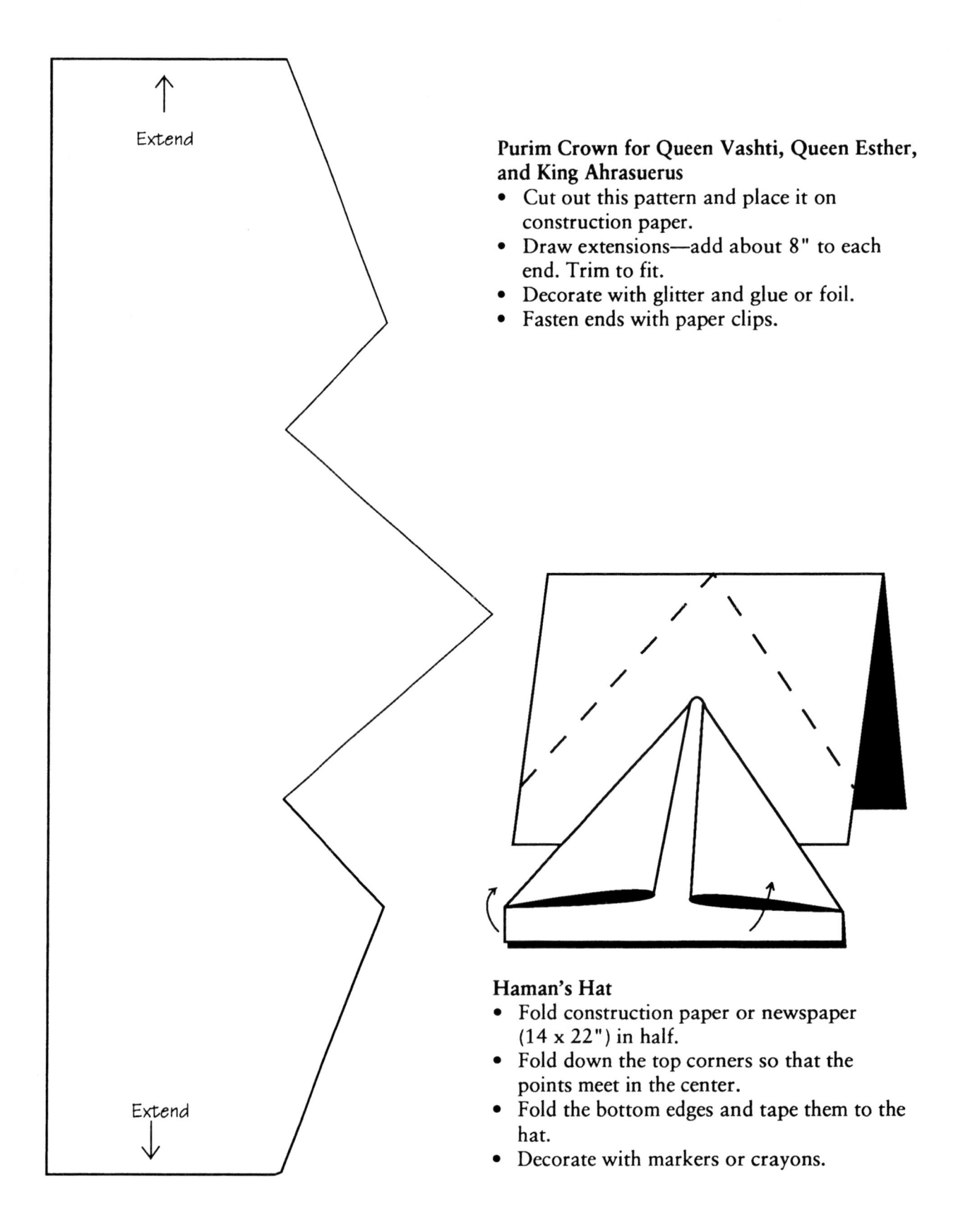

↑ Extend

Purim Crown for Queen Vashti, Queen Esther, and King Ahrasuerus
- Cut out this pattern and place it on construction paper.
- Draw extensions—add about 8" to each end. Trim to fit.
- Decorate with glitter and glue or foil.
- Fasten ends with paper clips.

Haman's Hat
- Fold construction paper or newspaper (14 x 22") in half.
- Fold down the top corners so that the points meet in the center.
- Fold the bottom edges and tape them to the hat.
- Decorate with markers or crayons.

Extend ↓

146 *Special Times* Unitarian Universalist Association

Lenten Letter to Participants and Parents

Dear

Next Sunday our *Special Times* group will talk about Lent. We will distribute Unitarian Universalist Service Committee (UUSC) "Guest at Your Table" boxes for the children (and families if you wish) to save money for UUSC projects around the world. We have enclosed a pamphlet explaining the UUSC and the "Guest at Your Table" project. We are suggesting that the children give up something to make this gift—part of their allowance, candy, or something your family decides together. Please have your child return the box on _____.
Thank you.

Peace,

Special Times Leaders

Enclosure: UUSC information on "Guest at Your Table" project

… RESOURCE 23

The Flaming Chalice Symbol

148 *Special Times* Unitarian Universalist Association

The Four Questions

Why do we eat matzoh on Pesa?

> Matzoh reminds us that when the Jews left Egypt, they had no time to bake bread for their journey. They put raw dough on their backs, and the sun baked it into hard crackers called matzoh.
>
> (Leader holds up the matzoh.)
> (All eat a small piece of matzoh and take a sip of juice.)

Why do we eat bitter herbs, maror, at the Seder?

> Maror reminds us of the bitter and cruel way Pharaoh treated the Jewish people when they were slaves in Egypt.
>
> (Leader holds up or points to the horseradish.)

Why do we dip foods twice at the Seder?

> We dip bitter herbs into charoset to remind us how hard the Jewish slaves worked in Egypt. The chopped apples and nuts look like clay which the Jews used to make bricks for building Pharaoh's cities and palaces.
>
> We dip parsley into salt water. The parsley reminds us that spring is here and new life will grow. The salt water reminds us of the tears of the Jewish slaves.
>
> (Leader dips the parsley in salt water.)

Why do we lean on a pillow at the Seder?

> We lean on a pillow to be comfortable and to remind us that once we were slaves, but now we are free.
>
> (All recline and partake of the food and juice.)

—from *My Very Own Haggadah,* by Judyth Saypol and Madeline Wikler. Copyright © 1974 by Kar-Ben Copies, Inc., Rockville, MD. For a free catalog call 1-800-4-KARBEN.

The Lord's Prayer

as interpreted by the Reverend Barbara Marshman

Our Father, who art in heaven. Hallowed be they name.

Giver of Life, who is in and beyond the universe, we would speak your name with thoughtfulness.

Thy kingdom come, thy will be done in earth as it is in heaven.

May we follow the laws of peace and understanding here on earth as the stars obey the laws of heaven.

Give us this day our daily bread.

May there be food for all so that none may go hungry.

And forgive us our trespasses as we forgive those who trespass against us.

When we have been unfair, unkind or thoughtless, give us the courage to say we are sorry and help us to be forgiving when others hurt us.

And lead us not into temptation but deliver us from evil.

Give us the strength to do what we feel is right and to turn away from whatever hurts ourselves or others.

For thine is the kingdom and the power and the glory forever and ever.

For the wonder, the beauty, and the goodness all around us we give praise and thanks.

Amen.

Easter Symbols

RESOURCE 26

Special Times   Unitarian Universalist Association   151

Star of David Pattern

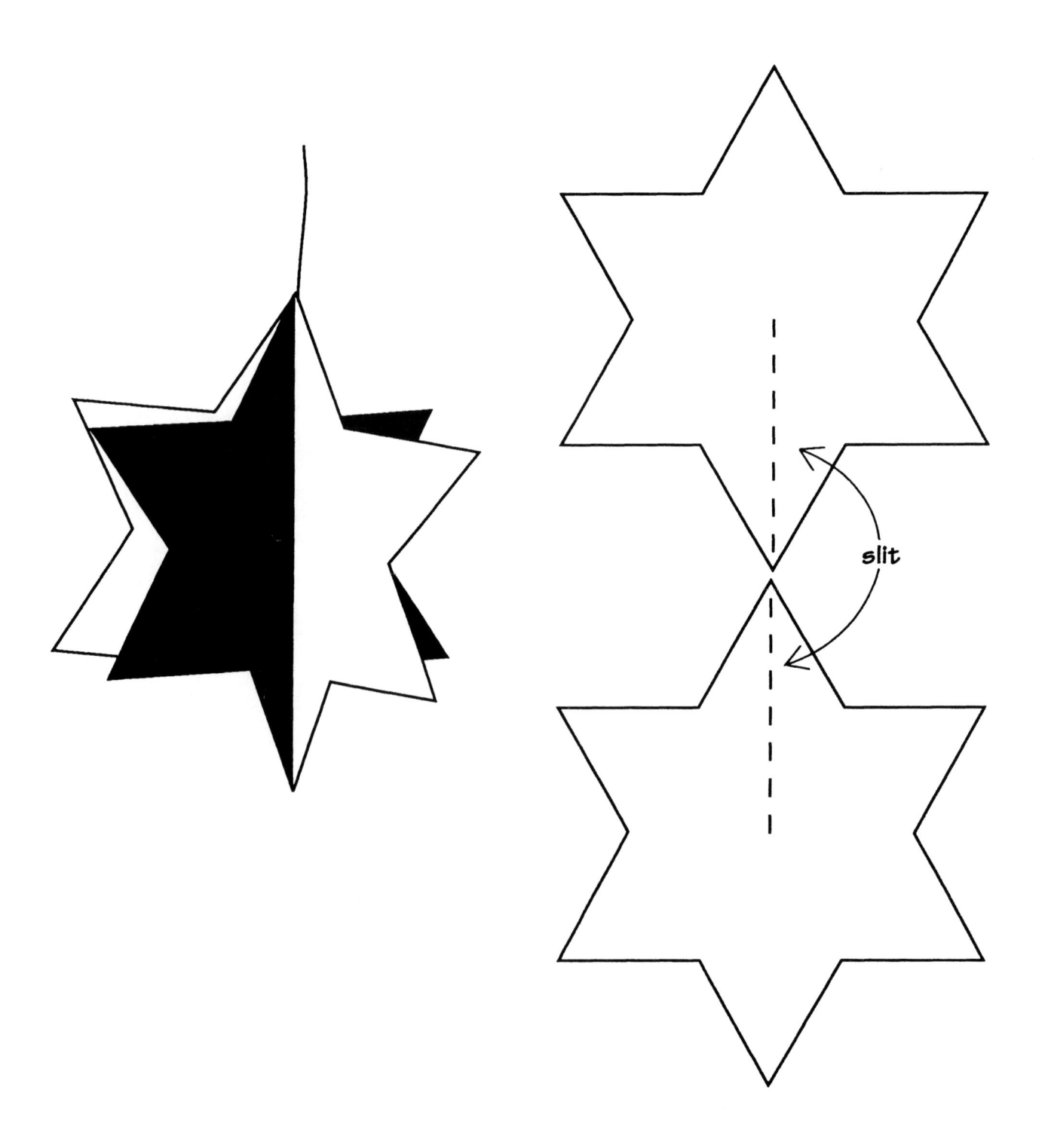

slit

152　　*Special Times*　　　　　　　　　　　　　Unitarian Universalist Association

The Ten Commandments

The Ten Commandments

1. You shall pray to only one God.

2. You shall not make yourself into a god.

3. You shall not say God's name with disrespect.

4. Celebrate Shabbat to remember that God rested on the seventh day.

5. Honor your father and mother.

6. You shall not murder.

7. Husband and wife shall not dishonor one another.

8. You shall not steal.

9. You shall not lie.

10. You shall not set your heart on having what others have.

—from *My Very Own Shavuot*, by Judyth Saypol and Madeline Wikler. Copyright © 1974 by Kar-Ben Copies, Inc., Rockville, MD. For a free catalog call 1-800-4-KARBEN.

Birthday Letter to Parents

Note: If you want to use postcards instead of letters, reduce this letter accordingly, or rewrite it to fit the format you're using.

Dear

Next Sunday we celebrate a time when each person is special—everybody's birthday! Please send or bring a baby picture of your child. We will return it after our celebration on Sunday.
    Thank you.

Shalom,

Special Times Leaders

Star Pattern

Special Times   **Unitarian Universalist Association**   155

Special Times Letter to Participants

Note: If you want to use postcards instead of letters, reduce this letter accordingly, or rewrite it to fit the format you're using.

Dear

This Sunday will be our final *Special Times* together. Think about the *Special Times* celebrations you have enjoyed the most. Please bring a white T-shirt. We will help you to decorate it with a *Special Times* design. A synthetic or synthetic blend T-shirt is best. You will be able to wash your shirt in the washer but will need to hang it to dry.

See you Sunday!

Shalom,

Special Times Leaders

Special Times Game Board

SABBATH

SHAVUOT	EASTER	YOM ha-ATZMAUT	ADVENT
LENT	ROSH HASHANAH	EPIPHANY	SUKKOT
PURIM	ALL SAINTS' DAY	CHRISTMAS	SIMHAT TORAH
ALL SOULS' DAY	PESAH	ST. VALENTINE'S DAY	YOM KIPPUR
TU BISHVAT	PALM SUNDAY	HANUKKAH	ST. FRANCIS' DAY

SHABBAT (left side)
SABBATH (right side)
SHABBAT (bottom)

RESOURCE 32

Special Times — Unitarian Universalist Association

Star of David, Cross, and Flaming Chalice Symbols

RESOURCE 33

158 *Special Times* Unitarian Universalist Association

Leader Evaluation Form for *Special Times*

We need you! Help us better serve your needs by sending us your comments, suggestions, and critiques of this program. Please photocopy this form, using additional sheets if needed, and send your evaluations to:

Unitarian Universalist Association
Curriculum Development Office
25 Beacon Street
Boston, MA 02108-2800.

General Information

1. With what age group did you use this curriculum?

2. Approximately how many participants were there?

3. How many leaders?

4. Is there anything else you would like to tell us about your religious education setting? (very small or very large congregation, etc.)

General Comments

It would be helpful if you would include comments on what worked, what didn't, and how you modified the program to fit your needs.